PERFECT COUNSELLING

Max A. Eggert
MA, BSc, AKC Psychol, FIPM, MITD

Max Eggert first read Theology before transferring
his allegiance to Psychology and then to Industrial
Relations.

He is Managing Partner of Eggert & Eggert, an
international consultancy dedicated to Human
Resources Management and Outplacement. Many
thousands of individuals at all levels and back-
grounds have benefited their careers by working
with Max who works in the UK and internationally
as a strategist and as an adviser to organizations
who retain his services.

OTHER TITLES IN THE SERIES

PERFECT COUNSELLING

All you need to get it right first time

Max Eggert

RANDOM HOUSE

BUSINESS BOOKS

This edition published in the United Kingdom in 1999
by Random House Business Books

2 4 6 8 10 9 7 5 3

First published in 1996 by Arrow Books Limited
The Random House Group Limited
20 Vauxhall Bridge Road, London, SWIV 2SA

Random House Australia (Pty) Limited
20 Alfred Street, Milsons Point,
Sydney, New South Wales 2061, Australia

Random House New Zealand Limited
18 Poland Road, Glenfield
Auckland 10, New Zealand

Random House (Pty) Limited
Endulini, 5a Jubilee Road, Parktown, 2193, South Africa

The Random House Group Limited Reg. No. 954009

Papers used by Random House are natural, recyclable
products made from wood grown in sustainable forests. The
manufacturing processes conform to the environmental regulations
of the country of origin

ISBN 0 09 940624 1

Companies, institutions and other organizations wishing to make
bulk purchases of any business books published by Random House
should contact their local bookstore or Random House direct:
Special Sales Director
Random House, 20 Vauxhall Bridge Road, London SW1V 2SA

Tel: 020 7840 8470 Fax: 020 7828 6681

www.randomhouse.co.uk
businessbooks@randomhouse.co.uk

Typeset in Sabon by SX Composing DTP, Rayleigh, Essex
Printed and bound in Norway by AIT Trondheim AS

This book is dedicated to three of the most significant women in my life:

Elizabeth – my beautiful mother who gave and encouraged my individuality

Heather – my beautiful partner, who cares and loves and indulges my individuality

Marisian – my beautiful daughter who loves me enough to ensure that my individuality does not go unchallenged

All of them have given me more wise counsel than I deserve or merit.

'Of course it was not I who cured. It was the power that came from the outer world, and the visions and the ceremonies had only made me like a hole through which power could come.'
    Black Elk

Contents

The counselling approach of this book

The emphasis in this book is on person-centred therapy, not because it is thought to be the most effective but because it is the most appropriate for those without the support of a strong psychological background. Our approach will be essentially in the tradition of Carl Rogers, whose methods enjoy built-in safety features for those who are new to counselling or for those who find themselves in counselling situations without the benefit of formal or advanced training. In person-centred therapy the counsellor, because of the emphasis on the relationship of both parties, moves with the client rather than being ahead of him and is not required to be in total control. It is not necessary for the counsellor to diagnose, deal with the unconscious, interpret dreams or even effect dynamic changes in personality, but rather to 'stay with' the person in pain and be part of the therapeutic process.

The relational emphasis of the Rogerian approach is neither complicated nor demands high intellectual rigour. The client is always the centre of attention, treated with genuine respect and positive regard. (See page 17.)

Those called upon immediately to help reduce the

pain of another, such as that brought about by bereavement, job loss, physical or sexual abuse, are not always the professionally trained counsellors but often the parent, friend, manager, nurse, doctor, policeman or cleric, any of whom can do much to relieve the pain of crisis by listening, hearing and understanding what the other person is experiencing at that particular time. Just being there for the person, sharing their pain, showing genuine care, concern and warmth can be immensely helpful. People in psychological pain or personal crisis can do without the easy platitudes of sympathy or the dictates of unfeeling authoritarianism but they do need the considerable benefits brought about by psychological contact, which is the touch-paper of most healing relationships. Simply – people in pain need 'someone who is there for them'.

The other thrust of the book comes from Brief Therapy which is pragmatic, parsimonious and will use whatever the client offers for the benefit of the therapeutic process. As in Rogerian therapy, Brief Therapy recognizes and emphasizes the strengths and resources of the client, rejoicing in the fact that most opportunities for change and change itself lie outside the counselling relationship, and that is more important than the therapy itself.

For many years counselling was thought to be the preserve of the professionals – psychologists, clinicians and therapists – yet everyone at some time in their life gets involved informally or even formally in counselling. The techniques, processes and skills of counselling are not in themselves difficult but being a good counsellor is far from easy because it is more to do with attitudes, beliefs, values and the world view of the counsellor.

This little book has essentially been written for non-professionals who find themselves in counselling

2

situations. It covers the main processes and skills used by the professionals. It is for managers, advisors, priests, nurses, police officers, social workers and, perhaps most of all, for parents – anyone who is called upon for help and support by another. People in need choose their counsellors and they do not always, because out of choice, finance, or anxiety, turn to 'the professionals'.

It is my hope that this book will help you to help others.

Max Eggert
Coogee South, New South Wales
April 1996

3

PART 1

Orientation towards counselling

THE COUNSELLING APPROACH

First, it is important to realize that counselling is not just a set of skills which can be strung together on a necklace of prescribed processes. As with most things it is not so much what you do but the way you do it. In counselling it is not only how you do it, but why you do it. This is because counselling has more to do with your individual approach and attitude towards others than the skills employed, important as these are. Approaching the individual in the right way and for the right reasons will, in terms of effectiveness and outcome, far surpass any skills say in questioning or attending, even though they are so germane to success. Perhaps this goes some way to explaining why it is that there is very little correlation between the intellectual capacity of the counsellor and counselling effectiveness and, indeed, why so many counsellors are 'chosen' by their clients. Unlike, say, a dentist or doctor and their patient, a counsellor and client usually have more of an interpersonal and intimate encounter/relationship which transcends the usual requirements and protocols required of the purely professional. In counselling, personal chemistry or synergy is almost as important as the skill portfolio and competence of the counsellor.

According to one study[1] good counsellors are not dissimilar to others in the caring professions, such as clergy and teachers, in that those who were perceived as being more effective hold as a cardinal value a commitment to a person-centred perspective. That is to say the individual in need has the total focus of the counsellor as well as the work they do together. So the good counsellor is more than someone with good interpersonal skills, he is someone who employs his skills from an expectation about the world and the people in it; he is able to see the world from perspectives other than his own with a passion for the general principle of wanting the best outcome for the client at all times. (See page 14 for the section on Unconditioned Positive Regard.)

This also prompts the 'why' of counselling. In Victorian times ladies ministered to women, thus satisfying the status needs of one group and the actual needs of the other. It is not too far from a parody to say that the way a Victorian female knew her role in society was whether or not she ministered or was ministered to. This is not to say that the 'ladies' did not possess genuineness, skills or personal qualities but rather their world view was 'I' centred rather than 'you' centred. There is nothing inappropriate about gaining satisfaction from helping individuals help themselves, but in the 'why' of counselling the individual in need is paramount.

[1] Coombs, A W, *What Makes a Good Helper?* Person-Centred Review 1:51-61 (1986)

COUNSELLING – A DEFINITION

Now we have examined some of the basic concepts around counselling it is possible to work towards a definition of what counselling might be. My own counselling began at work before moving into therapy and my own practice, which is why, in my early days, I found the following definition very helpful. It is based on the work of Barrie Hopson and provides a helpful starting point:

'*Counselling is assisting someone to explore and resolve difficulties they are experiencing, clarify conflicting issues and helping that person discover alternative ways of managing themselves and situations, so that they can decide what course of action or behaviour is helpful to them. Essentially it is helping people to help themselves.*'

This simple definition makes it clear that to counsel is to assist and not to direct; to help but not to take control; to encourage and support but not to take action. The individuality of the client and his capacity to play the most significant part in his own development, recovery or empowerment is paramount. As counsellors we are mere friends along the way. Someone once defined medicine as 'amusing' the patient whilst the body got on with the job of healing itself! Counselling has the same flavour – a theme to which we constantly return.

CONFIDENTIALITY AND CONFLICT

As counsellors we are privileged to be entrusted with the most sensitive and intimate information. Clients disclose to us things about themselves, their most private behaviours and their innermost thoughts, that they perhaps have not shared and would not dream of sharing with anyone else. We have a private conduit to the very soul of those with whom we work and thus there are the necessary protocols of confidentiality. The seal of the confessional would be the spiritual equivalent, not that we are secular priests, but the obligation on nondisclosure is almost the same. Perhaps the only exception is where the information given indicates the strong likelihood of danger or harm, either to the individual himself or to others.

Clients frequently come to us with moral quandaries and difficulties such as whether to remain in or separate from a relationship. Should I have this child? Should I declare that I'm gay? These are enormous questions for the client to live through and the innermost thoughts, personal values and beliefs of the individual need to be explored. With this degree of responsibility the imperative for confidentiality is as obvious as it is paramount.

Give the assurance of total confidentiality to your clients as early in your relationship with them as possible.

With these issues it is not surprising that we find in the 1984 guidelines from the British Association for Counselling the following five points:

- Counsellors treat with confidence personal information about clients, whether obtained directly or indirectly by inference. Such information includes name, address, biographic details, and other descriptions of the client's life and circumstances which might result in identification of the client.
- 'Treating with confidence' means not revealing any of the information noted above to any other person or through any public medium, except to those to

whom counsellors owe accountability for counselling work or on whom counsellors rely for support and supervision.

- Notwithstanding the above sections, if counsellors believe that a client could cause danger to others, they will advise the client that they may break confidentiality and take appropriate action to warn individuals or the authorities.
- Information about specific clients is only used for publications in appropriate journals or meetings with the client's permission and with anonymity preserved when specifics about the client are released.
- Counsellors' discussions of the clients with professional colleagues should be purposeful and not trivializing.

And it could be argued that this does not go far enough for some of the following could be useful additions:

- The client should be told and understand the confidentiality protocol and when it could be broken.
- Permission should always be gained, preferably in writing and certainly prior to the disclosure to another person or organization.
- Where information will be disclosed because of possible danger either to the client or to others, the client should be told of the disclosure before it is made.

COUNSELLING IS GOOD FOR YOU

Who benefits from the counselling process? Both parties, for it actually helps the counsellor in a variety of ways. It is difficult to help another unless you know and understand yourself, and the deeper that understanding of self, the more effective your counselling. Personal growth comes from within and through the process of helping others. We learn so much from our clients.

This is why all trainees in counselling are themselves counselled (this is called being under supervision). We develop ourselves in and through our relationship with others. Thus in working with others we develop a deeper understanding of ourselves.

The skills of the counsellor spill over into most other areas of life. In our daily lives it is beneficial to be able to get in and out of rapport, to listen and to interpret the behaviour of ourselves and others. This makes us more complete as individuals as well as enabling us to build deeper, more rewarding relationships. So being a counsellor brings a cornucopia of rewards as a parent, friend or partner.

You will discover that you learn so much from your clients and in helping them you also help yourself to resolve your own difficulties and problems, for none of us are exempt from the growing pains or vicissitudes of life.

Finally, there is the status that being a counsellor brings – improving your standing at work and in the community at large, increasing your confidence, bringing personal satisfaction and self-respect. It is wholesome to know that you are making an active and positive contribution to the wellness of humankind. In a world which is red in tooth and claw it is a noble privilege to care for another.

WHY PEOPLE COME FOR COUNSELLING

As hinted at already, why people come for counselling is best explained in the single word *pain*. It does not matter what the problem is, whether it be in terms of relational breakdown, physical trauma, lack of confidence, anxiety, fear or phobia, the client perceives their personal situation as painful.

Understanding the problem as 'pain' cuts a swath through much of the complex psychology and psychiatry associated with counselling. 'Pain' is very simple for both the counsellor and the client to understand. If you are committed to a certain school of psycho-dynamic approach because of your professional background there may be a danger of seeing and approaching problems in a specific way and delivering 'set' solutions to set problems, rather than dealing with your client's actual predicament.

When problems or difficulties are thought of as 'pain' for the client then we are more likely to undividualize our approach and our efforts are directed to the eradication and immediate cause, rather than trying to fit symptoms to a pertinent pathology. Nor is it likely that we will be sidetracked to work to a specific theory rather than dealing with the major presenting issue – the pain.

Clients, too, are more likely to be frank and open when talking about their 'pain', rather than their 'problem'. Pain is socially acceptable because it is universal, whereas problems are perceived in some way as having been brought about by the individual and can present the individual as in some way being inadequate.

Put simply, you are effective as a counsellor to the degree to which your client's pain is reduced. That is, can he now manage himself and his situation better – either through himself or resources which were not previously available? Elegant and ornate psycho-dynamic explanations of counselling are for case notes: they are not substitutes for effectiveness in the counselling relationship.

Ultimately it is the client who is in control of his own destiny and the outcomes of the counselling process. One of the fundamentals of counselling is that individuals have within them all that they need to overcome their problems. The counsellor then has to work to bring out those natural strengths and abilities. Black Elk, who is quoted at the beginning of the book, was absolutely right. This orientation highlights the difference between counselling and teaching. In the latter you are essentially supplying something which was not there before, but in counselling you assist the individual to fulfil their true selves by helping them discover the power and resources they *already* possess. No system yet has ever been devised whereby you could instruct an individual how to behave and/or feel in any given situation. Everyone responds differently. Very little needs to come from outside, for the individual holds all the resources for psychological and mental health.

Normality is the norm – problems, symptoms and pathology are barriers to normality, and they are 'worked through' rather than 'taught through'. We will return to this subject when we talk about empathy and positive regard. Perhaps this is why counselling is sometimes called the talking cure.

COUNSELLING IS ABOUT RESULTS

Much early work in psychotherapy and psychiatry was concerned with reasons and causality with great interest in the 'why' to account for an individual's difficulties. Present pain is obviously intimately connected with the past and one's subjective interpretation but, if we can use a medical model, knowing that I have a slipped disc from a riding accident in the past may satisfy my intellectual curiosity but far more important is the relief I now seek from my current pain. Which is the more appropriate: telling a starving mother that her condition is the result of minimal infrastructure and poor distribution, or giving her food? It is not so much about the 'why' (as interesting as that may be for prevention for self and others now and in the future) but the 'what' that can be done to relieve pain now. Aetiology can come later.

In this way counselling is a helping process – the 'ing' part of the word is very apposite because it reminds us that it is ongoing and continuous. Counselling rarely solves all the problems all at once. It is not like rebuilding a car engine where everything can be put right at once in a predetermined sequence. With counselling, individuals grow very slowly to manage their situation both in the present and in the future. Psychological archaeology for the individual is of interest, but by far the greatest impact is not the past, which is unchangeable, but the future with all its wonderful possibilities. Counselling helps people with the now and the future and in this way it should be results-orientated.

WHAT IS COUNSELLING?

Counselling is just one of many ways to help an individual. In counselling the emphasis is on the individual changing in some way so that they enjoy more control over themselves and their lives. As had been said before, this presupposes that the individual has the resources to make this possible.

In counselling there are two major components: the individual and the pain or the problem. Thus a way of identifying and understanding counselling is how these two aspects are approached.

Excludes the Client

Telling	**Manipulating**

Problem   Client

Focused   Focused

Advising	**Counselling**

Includes the Client

Fig 1

As can be clearly seen from figure 1, how you approach the problem and the individual suggests different ways of helping. In counselling we want to be client focused and include the client as much as possible.

If you are more concerned about the problem and its resolution and just anticipate the client passively accepting your solution, then the main activity is that of **telling**, not counselling.

Even if you include the client but are still mainly focused on the problem, then this activity is that of **advising**, not counselling.

Telling and advising as methods of getting people to change their behaviour are notoriously ineffective. If they worked, none of us would smoke, drink and drive, or eat junk food. **Counselling** is more likely to achieve more permanent changes in behaviour.

Again looking at figure 1, of course it is possible to focus on the client as an entity and not as a person. Doctors do this when they diagnose an illness. You are asked a whole string of questions, almost as if you are a car in for a service. It is an effective way of identifying the physical illness very quickly. If this approach of concentrating on the individual without including him or her is used in counselling it is more likely to be **manipulation** than counselling. It is getting them unknowingly to behave in a way which benefits the other person.

Finally, when you are client focused and including the client as an equal in the process then it is more likely to be considered **counselling**.

So this brings us back to our earlier definition of counselling. Counselling is supporting a person whilst they explore a current difficulty or problem, clarifying conflicting issues and helping them to discover alternative behaviours and ways of dealing with their situation, so that the person themselves can decide what they wish to do; essentially counselling is assisting people to help themselves.

Several assumptions become apparent when we think through this definition.

- Individuals know themselves better than anyone else.
- Individuals know what they really want and orientate their behaviour to satisfy their perceived needs.
- Individuals have the ability to decide for themselves how they wish to behave.
- Individuals have the resources within them to achieve what they want.

Looking and thinking about counselling in this way highlights the significant differences between counselling as a developmental process and teaching or coaching.

Throughout counselling, the client always owns his problems, the alternatives and the decisions which are available to him. These are not taken away or solved by the counsellor nor does the counsellor abrogate the individual's responsibility. Interventions are perhaps the closest that the counsellor comes to taking direct action but even then the client has the choice to participate or reject what is being suggested. Compliance with the counsellor is not a common concept or expectation as it would be in teaching or coaching an individual, where doing as you are told is usually a prerequisite for success and there are penalties for non-compliance.

THE COUNSELLING PARTNERSHIP

Counselling is not something which is 'done' to another person but rather something that two or more people engage in doing together. Yes, the role of the client is different to the role of the counsellor. For the process to be effective those involved must come together as co-workers in a team. Various attempts have been made to explain this concept. 'Mutual empowerment', 'partnership' and 'mutuality' have all been suggested and each of them gives the flavour and feel. It is really difficult in real life situations to establish this required equality because of predetermined roles or situations which push the relationship into being asymmetric, i.e. one person has more power or authority than the other. For example, nurse and patient, father and son, manager and subordinate. Previous power roles between the parties tend to mitigate against moves towards equality. Even the terms counsellor and client suggests this underlying theme of authority, especially when clients 'go' to a counsellor, in his or her office, at a time and duration determined by the counsellor for a session set by the counsellor.

Yet one of the key skills for the counsellor is to use

his expertise to best serve the needs of the client. And this is not easy, for I have spent years training to reach my position as a counsellor and it is hard to give the power back to the client who has not had the benefit of such training. And, because of my experience and previous successes, I am confident about what needs to be done 'to effect a cure', and thus the client's compliance is more welcome than his participation.

Yet, it is through the quality of relationships that both counsellor and client become empowered to blossom and become their true selves in the world.

It is within relationships that we discover our sameness and also how we are different and this draws us to conclusions about our individuality. We know who we are through our relationships. It is only in true and full relationships that affections and feelings can be reciprocated. To love and be loved, to help and be helped is the essence of our humanity and can only be gained through mutual respect and valuing. Finally, it is where we share common ideas and interests with others that partnership and mutuality can make their significant contribution to the healing process. Hence, the quality and nature of the relationship is critical for successful counselling.

Carl Rogers working in the 1940s suggested what are perhaps now the most widely accepted 'core conditions' for the counselling process. These are so important in underpinning any counselling relationship, skills aside, that there will be a section on each of them. They are:

GENUINENESS

UNCONDITIONAL POSITIVE REGARD

EMPATHY

CONGRUENCE OR GENUINENESS

For Rogers 'genuineness', certainly in his later writings, was the most important aspect in the counselling relationship. It means simply that in the relationship the counsellor must be primarily himself, as a real person: genuine, authentic and integrated. What he feels and the way he appears should be one and the same; openly expressing himself, and his current feelings and attitudes. This means not hiding behind a professional façade of 'I am the counsellor, you are the client' but more an 'I/thou' relationship of two people coming together honestly and openly in a relationship of mutual respect and trust. If the counsellor cannot be open and honest as a person with the client, how can it be expected of the client? If genuineness is missing, what hope is there for the potential therapeutic process.

A useful list of behaviours that would suggest genuineness of the counsellor are:[2]

- Not emphasizing the helping role
- Being spontaneous
- Not being defensive
- . Consistency
- Being open
- Being comfortable with processes which help the client

Counsellors as well as clients have feelings and it is acceptable to make them manifest during the counselling session. Where feelings are ignored or stifled, the counsellor becomes incongruent and not genuine as a

[2] Egan, G, *The Skilled Helper*, 4th Edition. Monterey (1990)

person. In this impoverished state he is unable to deliver fully what is needed for the therapeutic process.

Essentially, it is a balancing act with the counsellor acting as the fulcrum. Sessions should not be overloaded with their feelings and preoccupations, but nor should they be locked away from the client.

How the counsellor feels and behaves should be the same: this is being congruent. As with most behaviours, being congruent is not either/or nor 'all or nothing', but operates on a scale or a continuum. Rather like Goldilocks' porridge, a counsellor's emotions and feelings should not be too hot or too cold, but 'just right'.

UNCONDITIONAL POSITIVE REGARD

Counsellors must show complete commitment and care for their clients as unique individuals. This caring comes without any preconditions. There are no bargains, deals or limitations placed upon the client, not are the client's behaviour, thoughts or feelings evaluated as good or bad, just accepted. The counsellor approaches the client as someone who is entitled to feelings and to their unique experiences, perceptions and judgements without fear of losing the counsellor's positive regard. Some behaviours are, of course, unacceptable to the counsellor but even in these rare circumstances his attitude towards the client should remain positive – the behaviour is not acceptable but the person is.

Rogers[3] suggests that the greatest acceptance possible can be thought of as 'prizing' or 'valuing' the client

[3] Rogers, C, *Carl Rogers on Personal Power: Inner Strength and its revolutionary impact*, New York, Delacaster Press (1970)

in a non-possessive way. The greater the 'prizing', the better chance of achieving a successful outcome.

Person perception is not the preserve of the psychologist or the professional; most clients can recognize whether or not they are being accepted for what they are by the counsellor. When this is missing, clients usually become more defensive and less co-operative in the process.

EMPATHY

Empathy is frequently confused with sympathy or feeling sorry for the client, when it is actually understanding the client's feelings and experiences as they are shared in each moment of the session. It is keeping in the 'here and now', the constant present, endeavouring to feel what the client is going through. The objective of this is so the client can get close to their own current feelings and thereby recognize and resolve any incongruity that they experience.

Obviously, the counsellor does not lose control, suffocated by the client's intensity, but shares enough of the emotions so that the client appreciates that the counsellor knows their pain. The counsellor can then use this knowledge of the pain to help unfold meaning and understanding for the client.

Empathy is not about knowledge – 'I know how you feel', but about personal experience with the client – 'I feel what you feel'. Where the counsellor can enter the client's world, without forsaking his or her own individual identity, then constructive change will commence.

Ideally, empathy should be mutual with both sides giving and receiving warmth, respect and genuineness, but where this is not possible it is the responsibility of the counsellor to understand the client and for the client to feel understood.[4]

Cautionary Note:
Some clients find this Rogerian approach too personal and intimate, in which case it may be helpful to become a little more formal and distant in your relationship.

WHAT MAKES A CLIENT

Strange as it may seem, not everyone who presents themselves or is referred as a client actually *is* one. Rather like, not everyone who walks into a shop is a buyer. People enter shops for a whole host of reasons other than wanting to buy something. They may come into the shop out of curiosity, to kill time, look good, indulge in fantasy, window shop, meet friends, to steal or just to get out of the rain. The wise shopkeeper will have scenarios for all these contingencies.

In counselling there are basically three categories of clients:

True Clients
True clients recognize that they are in a situation which they wish to improve/change and demonstrate a commitment to personal action. True clients are those who see themselves as an inseparable part of the counselling.

Plaintives or Complainers
Plaintives or Complainers recognize that a difficulty

[4] Crompton, M, *Children and Counselling*, Edward Arnold (1992)

does exist but they are outside the situation. Sometimes it is difficult and takes several sessions to differentiate True clients from Plaintives, for the latter are often in pain or distress because of their situation, but through discussion it becomes apparent that they see any causality with their predicament or responsibility for helping lying *outside* themselves. They are the injured party and it is others that need sorting out. Essentially, it is not their problem.

In such cases it is not the role of the counsellor to employ his or her skills to effect a change in someone who does not wish it. It is rather like the mother in the park who says, dictatorially, to her disgruntled child, 'I brought you here to enjoy yourself and enjoy yourself you will.'

Visitors
Thirdly, there are Visitors – of which there are two types. There are those who do not even recognize there is a problem. Usually they are sent by a third party. The potential client has their mind set that nothing is wrong and his or her presence is to fulfil an obligation to a superior or a moral obligation to a family member. A line manager might 'send' someone down to Personnel because of his interpersonal behaviour, a colonel might set one of his men to the chaplain for a chat, a mother might send her daughter to a therapist about her sexual activities, but in each case the person who is 'sent' feels their behaviour or values are normal and everyday.

Finally, there are Visitors who are curious or fashion conscious. They have no real problem but seeing a counsellor is the 'thing to do'. Or a particular counsellor may take on a sort of cult status where it is perceived as prestigious to be seeing this particular person. I remember being at The Tavistock in London for group sessions and one participant had come mainly because 'all her friends had been' so she wanted to participate, thus keeping up psychologically with the Joneses.

Obviously it is only with True clients that real work can be done.[5] Sometimes Plaintives realize they are the 'only person in the platoon who is in step' and make the transition to True client. Visitors too are difficult, especially if they are referred by society through the courts or some other system.

SOME DIFFICULTIES WITH COUNSELLING

Obviously this book is not intended to put you off counselling before you start, but it is as well to be aware of some of the difficulties because 'forewarned is forearmed'. As you will discover, some of these difficulties overlap one with another. There are four main areas of danger:

Role Conflict: You, the Client and the Institution
As a priest, police officer, nurse or doctor you have a professional role in your organization. Sometimes what is in the best interests of the individual you are counselling does not coincide with the best interests of your organization and this causes conflict. Literature, films and plays abound with this conflict as a plot. Are you true to your profession or to your client? What happens when you are a junior HR person with responsibility for reducing absenteeism and one of your employees comes to you with problems that obviously require him or her to be at home? How do you balance your conflicting

[5] de Sharze, S, *Clues: Investigating Solutions in Brief Therapy*, New York, Norton (1988)

22

responsibilities, one to your employer and the other to the employee who is now your client?

Conflict of Confidentiality

For counselling to work it requires frankness and truth, but what happens when this truth has serious implications outside the counselling situation? Confessions of child abuse, physical vengeance, expressed suicide wishes, although not frequent will occur at some time.

Possessiveness and Competence

Sometimes counsellors become over-possessive about their clients, seeing clients as wholly theirs and themselves as in some way indispensable to their improvement. This is one of the many reasons why supervision (see page 9) is so important so that counsellors can review themselves and their clients in perspective.

Occasionally, because of possessiveness or because helpful and caring people step in 'where angels fear to tread', they find themselves with situations which are far too complex or complicated psychologically or emotionally for them to deal with. To a certain extent the client shares part of the responsibility for this situation since he chooses to unburden himself to you, but this is not always the case. Sometimes individuals are in so much pain and distress that the first available person with ears is deemed the counsellor. Even so, you must recognize and work to your limitations and not feel inadequate if you think it best to refer your new client on to someone with more skill or experience than yourself.[6]

[6] Dryden, W, *A Dialogue with Arnold Lazarus*, Open University Press (1991)

The Forbidden Zone

Clients come to counsellors when they are highly vulnerable, anxious and in need of empathy, care and support. When this is generously given by the counsellor his behaviour can be misinterpreted as showing affection for the client, who may then respond accordingly, as inappropriate as this may be.

This process is well known but as a counsellor you should take care and be aware that your care and concern may be interpreted as an invitation to a relationship – far different from that of counsellor/client. Also, be aware of your own positive or negative feelings towards the client.[7]

HOW TO APPROACH COUNSELLING

Be Yourself

Being yourself with your clients is far more important than playing the role of counsellor. Theory and techniques are very important and need to be mastered, but then you have to go with the flow and be yourself. Rather like a 'work to rule' would seize up any organization, so if you hold yourself back your counselling will be impoverished.

Over-rigorous efforts to apply either theory or technique will mean missing the opportunity to deliver care from your unique personality, experience and the needs of the moment. One psychotherapist put it thus, 'what this profession needs is a good dose of non-theory.'[8]

[7] Winnicott, D N, 'Hate in the Counter Transference', *Int. J. Of Psychoanalysis* 30.194 ff (1949)
[8] Neill and Kniskern, *From Psyche to System: The Evolving Therapy of Carl Whitaker*, New York, Guilford (1982)

It is a balance and a medium – at one end there is the professional façade and at the other end there is the 'look at me I'm a person too'. Being professional in counselling is not to be an automaton or a buddy buddy but to be yourself, using the tools and strategies of your trade in the way you feel they will contribute to the welfare of the client.

Be practical rather than perfect

Humans are so wonderfully created and so complex that there are no absolute or right ways. If Freud had been totally effective there would have been no need for Jung or Adler. If Person-Centred therapy was the right method there would be no need for Gestalt therapy, Transactional analysis or Behaviour therapy. Each approach makes a contribution, but none is perfect.

As in life, so in counselling – you get things right by getting them wrong. Not that anyone wants to fail deliberately but, when working with individuals, set pieces never bring set results. It was once said 'Ignorance never prevented the practice of medicine', this is also true for counselling. Errors, whilst not deliberate, are inevitable but bring with them greater learning opportunities.[9]

THE DANGERS OF BURN-OUT

If you do a lot of counselling then burn-out is a real possibility. Counselling is essentially about giving and you

[9] Kottler and Blau, *The Imperfect Therapist*. 'Learning from Failure in Therapeutic Practice' San Francisco, Jossey-Bass (1989)

can only give so much before you need to recuperate. Not 'recharging your batteries' will make you 'flat' and you will be no good to yourself or to others.

A large combination of factors can bring about burn-out, reflecting the individual, interpersonal, environmental and organizational aspects which come together to bring about the condition.

Here are some of the causes:

- giving much and not receiving appreciation
- doing work which gives minimum results and appears to have little meaning
- working with involuntary, antagonstic clients
- not appearing to achieve any beneficial results from clients
- not being able to learn or try anything new where experimentation and innovation are actively repressed.
- being under constant pressure or being expected to meet unrealistic deadlines or targets
- lack of trust with superiors, peers or subordinates
- performing similar work to strict procedures
- external problems to the job such as health, domestic or finance

Some people in the caring professions are more susceptible to burn-out, especially those who want to care because feeling needed is very important to them or they have strong need for approval.

Consequently, it is important for you to take personal stock on a regular basis and certainly your own well-being should be a definite agenda item for yourself and your supervisor.

REJOICING IN SLOW RESULTS

One always has to remember that most people have spent a lifetime investing in their behaviour, habits, values and beliefs and so it is difficult for them to give up such a hard-earned investment lightly – even if it is in their long-term interest.

In physics and engineering there is a term, 'historesis', which, in simple terms, means that when a substance is compressed into a new shape there is always a tendency for that new shape to revert back to its original configuration. Clients share this same tendency. One only has to look at the difficulty when attempting to change our own behaviours and habits or being faithful to the new commitments we make to ourselves. Slippage is to be expected.

It should also be remembered that in counselling 'it gets worse before it gets better'. Anyone who attempts to change their behaviour encounters difficulties in the learning and development of new habits. Just as a baby who begins to walk falls regularly and will frequently revert to crawling, so someone who attempts to change behaviour also 'falls over' and sometimes finds it easier to return to his old ways.

NOT GIVING ADVICE

Because you will find yourself frequently dealing with similar problems for your clients it will not be long before you build up a well-stocked store of methods and ways of resolving these 'typical' and commonly recurring difficulties. Even before the client has finished speaking you might find yourself anticipating what they are going to say next and what their difficulties are. So the danger is the urge to launch yourself into automatic-solutions-mode, moving from a *counselling* to a *telling* orientation and even sometimes into selling the client solutions. Clients themselves are not participating in this process. If most human difficulties could be solved by just telling people what to do, the world would be almost perfect overnight, because we would all be taking instructions from those who were more knowledgeable, wiser than ourselves or who had specific professional skills. There is a huge gap between listening and behaviour and – not surprisingly – that gap is filled by the personality, needs and intellect of the client who, in a real sense, has to participate in the process.

Helping another through counselling is very much a team effort. Essential to the process are both the counsellor and the client (with most of the work being done by the client), and that is why it takes a long time. Telling or giving advice have their place when there is a technical enquiry or problem. If someone wants to change a wheel, mend a puncture, or wants to know what bus to catch, going into counselling mode is about as welcome as a cockroach at a picnic. The person needs to know 'what to do', but in counselling most people also want to know 'how to do', and the two are essentially different. The 'what' is about things and facts: the 'how' is about processes and people. Thus telling or advising people what to do because 'if I were you, I would' is not as powerful as helping individuals to work out 'how to do' for themselves. They are both critical and intrinsic to the counselling process – for responsibility for actions and behaviours always belongs to the client.

There is a game which some clients play called 'total compliance'. It is quite a simple game in that the client is either given advice or manoeuvres until advice is given by the counsellor. That advice is followed absolutely and to the letter and then, when the results are less that satisfactory, the client who is blameless blames the counsellor because 'I did exactly as I was told.'

PART 2

The basic skills of counselling

COUNSELLING SKILLS

In this section we examine the basic skills of counselling and we shall cover:

- How to attend a person – How to welcome the person into the social interaction.
- How to ask questions – If we can ask the right questions and question in the right way, both the client and ourselves will gain the benefit of the information we both need to move forward.
- How to listen – It is one thing to get information but another to actually capture it.
- How to get into rapport – How to attend an individual so that you can relate to them in a satisfactory manner and terminate the relationship appropriately.
- Managing the process – How to move an individual forward in the counselling processes.
- Strategies, tactics and tips – How to use tried and tested techniques of counselling.

In real life all the skills merge and integrate into one

another. They are divided here for the sake of convenience.

ATTENTING SKILLS

When someone seeks your help the first skill is to attend to them as a person. This is 'body listening' as opposed to 'hearing listening'. As every parent with a teenager will know from experience it is possible to hear someone and yet not attend to them. Attending shows the other person that they are important and that they are of significance to you. We can show through the use of our bodies what we think of another person, whether we invite someone into a personal relationship or 'turn our back on them'.

Skills of attending are obvious – just treat the person as if they were special and important to you. Here is a suggestion to help you attend to another person when counselling them. Try it and perfect it in your day-to-day social situations first, but I am sure you will find it helpful with your clients.

Float
F: Face the person – your shoulders should be parallel with those of the person with whom you are working. We turn away from people we do not like, give them 'the cold shoulder'. In Victorian times ladies of a superior station in life would 'cut' those whom they thought beneath them. The 'cut' was physically turning away and pretending those of presumed lesser rank were not there.
L: Lean toward the person. This is a natural response – when you want to hear someone, you move towards them. It shows that the person is the centre of

attention and you want to 'catch' everything they say, you want to be involved with them.

O: Open yourself to the other person, accept who they are and that what they say is important. This can be shown physically by not crossing your arms or legs even though this might be comfortable for you. (When in a chair without armrests for any length of time the act of crossing your arms can be quite comfortable but experts in body language tell us we are sending out a message that we are trying to protect ourselves.) Nor is it helpful to hide behind large note pads or clipboards.

A: Attend to the person – look at them and give them your absolute attention. Because people communicate with their faces and the rest of their bodies so much more than with the words that come out of their mouths, you have to attend to the person completely to understand them. Watch good friends enjoy a conversation – they naturally look at each other. Eye contact converts the sound of speech into the reality of communication.

T: Track the person – what are they saying? What do they mean? How do they feel about what they are saying and what is their current state of feelings? That is staying with your client wherever they take you.

By using these simple courtesies you will communicate to the client how important they are, that they are significant and valued as individuals.

Make sure that your seating arrangements are not only comfortable, but that both of you are at the same level. Do not use the ploy of royalty or the judiciary ensuring that your seat is highest in the room so that your clients must 'look up' to you. Remove any physical barriers between you, such as desks or high tables. Not only do these make sessions more formal, they make it difficult to pick up on body language. When we are anxious it is surprising how much our legs and feet do the talking.

DEVELOPING RAPPORT

Not everyone can launch into their difficulty or 'open up' to you immediately, and it is important to begin with the normal, non-threatening conversations of everyday life. Comments on the weather, journey and the offering of tea or coffee should not be undervalued. Clients have enough anxiety dealing with their problems and do not need this exaggerated by coming to a strange place where the system and the protocols are unclear. With a little thought much can be done to reduce 'service anxiety' i.e. apprehension about meeting you on your home territory, so that you can get on with dealing with 'problem anxiety'.[10]

ASKING QUESTIONS

Questions have a number of uses in counselling. First of all they can promote discussion and rapport. They help you gain and discover information that both you and your client require. Questions can also be employed to promote mental activity around the topic, problem or difficulty, so that the client can think things through using a different perspective. Questions can be quite challenging and resolutions can be achieved by thinking through the problem or difficulty in a new light.

[10] Howe, D, *The Consumer's View of Family Therapy*, Gower (1989)

Questions also bring clarification when you are not clear about what the client is saying.

The most powerful questions are called 'open' questions, that is those questions that cannot be answered with just a 'Yes' or 'No'. Open questions usually begin with:

> What
> Why*
> When
> Who
> How

The advantage of the open question is that it gives no limit of how you wish it to be answered. So, for instance, 'Do you feel well?' is not as powerful a question as 'How do you feel?' The open question elicits far more information from the client than the closed question 'Do you feel well?' You can see that questions such as:

> 'What prompted you to seek counselling?'
> 'What do you expect from counselling?'
> 'How will you know you are making progress?'

are powerful questions and are impossible to answer with a straight 'Yes' or 'No'. Such questions encourage clients to think through various answers they could give and their answer then has to be given a format and structure. Sometimes, as they think through possible alternative answers, solutions to their difficulties or problems are generated almost of their own accord.

You may have noticed that in the above list 'Why' is given an asterisk. This is because 'Why?' can be fraught with problems. If you ask 'Why?' you usually get a rationalization rather than the true answer. If you want to

use 'Why' then preface it with a softening statement.
Here are some examples:

'That is interesting, why was that?'
'Oh really, can you tell me why?'
'I can see that, why?'

Using the softening statement somehow takes the
inquisitional edge off the 'Why'.

Open questions are excellent at establishing rapport
and gaining opinions from clients, but there are some
more sophisticated ways of gaining information.

Para language
'Ums' and 'ahs' in the right places help clients to expand
on what they are saying. They tell the client that you
have listened and would like to know more. You might
feel a bit silly saying 'um' or 'ah' but most people don't
hear them in their conscious listening. Rather like subliminal perception where things are seen but not noticed,
your 'ums' are heard but not listened to.

Suggestive Statements
This is like para language, but uses words that have little
relevant meaning. Common statements include:

'Oh really'
'I see'
'Exactly'
'Fascinating'
'You don't say'
'Good'
'Excellent'
'So?'
'Yes'

'And?'

Again, the purpose of suggestive statements is to encourage the client to go on talking, expanding or amplifying the point he is making.

Mirror Statements

This is where you take what the client has said and rephrase it back to him, rather like holding up a verbal mirror which reflects back what is said as closely as possible. Here is an example:

Client: 'I have a really difficult manager. He shouts at me and I get intimidated.'
You: 'You have a problem with your boss who is aggressive and you become frightened?'

Mirror statements show that you are listening to the person and encourage them to go on.

Key Word Repetition

By listening to the client you take the key word from what he has just said and reflect it back to him. So in the example above again:

Client: 'I have a really difficult manager. He shouts at me and I get intimidated.'
You: 'Intimidated?'
Client: 'Yes, it is very frightening, especially when I'm in the office on my own.'
You: 'On your own?'

Although you might feel a bit of a parrot, you will be surprised how much additional information this generates from clients.

The Pause or Silence

Just by staying quiet invites the client to say more, providing it is not an oppressive silence. Silence allows both parties time to think and reflect on what *has* been said, and what *could* be said and what *should* be said. Silence also facilitates rapport between you.

Normally it will be the client who breaks the silence unless you feel resentment on behalf of the client, in which case you can make a process statement and move on. For example, after a prolonged silence you might comment: 'You seem to have said all you want to on that subject'.

There is some evidence to show that natural pauses are culturally determined and it is wise to follow or pace your pauses in sync with your client.[11]

Other Types of Questions

Sometimes it is useful to use 'comparative' questions, such as:

'How do you feel you have changed?'

or

'What is different now?'

in that they promote an internal dialogue in the client. On other occasions 'hypothetical questions' can be used to advantage, especially when you wish to help clients reflect and consider options available to them. For example:

[11] Tannen, D, *That's not what I meant!*, London, Virago (1992)

'What would happen if . . .?'
'If you did that, what might be the result?'
'When do you think you might do that?'

Certain types of questions are not helpful, such as those which push the client in a particular direction.

'You do want . . . don't you?'
'It would be good to . . . wouldn't it?'

These 'leading questions' are very helpful in a counselling context.

LISTENING

We perhaps spend more time listening than any other conscious human activity apart from seeing and thinking. We are surrounded by conversation, information and the noise of the world. It is not surprising that in a world flooded with sound, research suggests only about 25 per cent of what we hear actually registers with us. It has always surprised me that at school there was always an emphasis on reading skills but I cannot remember ever being taught to listen – it was taken as read! When we were told to pay attention and listen, I recall that what we were supposed to do was to sit up straight like a ramrod, which was difficult for me since I was used to sitting comfortably to listen to stories at home with my parents.

Hearing is a physiological function and listening is a psychological activity, and the two are completely different. My children could always repeat almost verbatim what I was saying when challenged, but I knew and they knew that they weren't listening. My father would read the paper and have a conversation consisting of 'yes', 'no, 'really', 'you don't say' with my mother most evenings.

Listening is one of the skills of counselling. You can infer what someone is saying or feeling by their demeanour and body language, but it is only by listening to them that you gain information about how they feel, and what is happening inside their emotional and psychological world.

'It is surprising what you hear when you listen'

WHY IS LISTENING DIFFICULT?

Basically, the brain works very much faster than the mouth. Consequently, because language is delivered so slowly and sequentially, well below the processing capacity of the brain, the brain frequently goes 'walk about' whilst we are listening. Also, what it finds when it does go walk about is sometimes more interesting and it does not come back! Here are some of the more common difficulties:

Self talk
When someone talks to us, we continually challenge ourselves by asking questions of ourselves such as 'Is that right?', 'Is that credible?', 'Does that make sense?', 'What is she really trying to say?', 'Do I believe her?' Then this self-debate which is triggered from outside gets taken into the head and, of course, as soon as that happens we are having conversations in our head and not listening. In my seminars I ask for a show of hands of those people in the group who 'talk to themselves in their head'. Usually about two-thirds of the hands go up

immediately and to the remainder I say, to the amusement of all, 'you're asking yourself – do I have conversations in my head or don't I?'

Personal planning

Most of us have personal priorities and commitments and sometimes we catch ourselves wandering outside the conversation with clients to those personal aspects of our lives – 'I wonder what the children are doing?', 'Will I finish early tonight?', 'Have I remembered to feed the cat?', 'Have I paid my credit card bill?', and the thousand and one of life's little things that need to be done. Counsellors are human too, with anxieties and difficulties of their own. Often the client will say something which strikes a chord within us and we are away thinking about our own world. Suddenly we realize that we have missed what the client is saying – rather like driving on the motorway and suddenly realizing that you have just driven ten miles without being able to remember actually driving. There is the old joke about the psychiatrist who, when asked 'How can you spend all your time listening to people day after day?' replies 'Who listens?'

Distractions

Anyone who has had a session with a client on a hot summer afternoon after lunch will know it is difficult for both parties to stay awake. Temperature, time of day, noises, how comfortable or otherwise the seating arrangements are, the decor, pictures and a hundred and one other things in the environment will act as distractions for both yourself and your client. One of my clients would regularly start her session by asking if she could straighten the pictures in the consulting room, another would attempt to read (from his position it would be upside-down) everything on my desk. I have a habit of straightening my pens and having them as close to 90° to the edge of the table as possible. I was not even conscious I did this until an ex-client mentioned how distracting it was as she thought I was more interested in my pens being tidy than in her, whilst it was my intention to put my pen down to give her maximum attention!

Difficult listening

Sometimes the client is difficult to understand because of an impediment, an accent or even the subject matter. Listening is hard work – if I can paraphrase Yogi Berra 'It is surprising what you hear when you listen'. All that the client discloses, as we will discover later with the skills of listening, is significant for it gives us clues not only to the current difficulties but also to solutions.

Emotional interference

As a rule of thumb for myself I find about 20 per cent of the human race very attractive and I enjoy their company very much. About 60 per cent are acceptable, for me these people are OK, I would not choose them as close friends but I could certainly work quite well with them irrespective of whether they were my manager, my colleague, my subordinate or my client. However, the remaining 20 per cent I do have difficulty working with because for some reason we don't get on – there is no 'synergy'. Now I can be polite, well-mannered and keep it under control by falling back on learned rapport skills, but it does not alter the fact that I find these people difficult to listen to because of the emotional interference. So with this group I work doubly hard to ensure they get my total concentration, for it is critical for them (and for my professionalism) that they have my total positive regard (see page 18), and are valued just as much as those people I do enjoy working with. However, there is a self-selection process in such matters because clients usually gravitate to counsellors they like or think they can work with, or who will be sympathetic to their situation. (Yes, sympathetic, not empathetic.)

Prejudice

Similar to emotional interference I am prejudiced at deep level against people who are not akin to me in terms of my culture, background and even colour and gender. My feelings were imprinted before I was old enough to know about the necessity and beauty of equality and multiculturalism. I work exceptionally hard at not showing myself up in either language or action, but I know it is still there just below the surface. It happens before I know it, especially when I first meet someone. I have put them in one of my stereotype boxes with the lid almost secured down before I bring myself up sharp and remind myself that we are all victims of our physical attributes. If you are not careful you find yourself listening to what you expect to hear, and expectations create reality. Isolated utterances that fit the stereotype are remembered while all the rest somehow just fade away and we miss the real person. When we only see and hear what we want to, prejudice is perpetrated.

PERSONAL LIMITATIONS

We can only really understand fully that which we have experienced ourselves. If we have not experienced an event it is difficult to comprehend it in any way as we have no context or background. It is said that the natives of the West Indies, when they first saw the three ships of

Columbus, thought they were not sea vessels but clouds. When the natives of Central America first saw the men of Cortez on horseback they thought they were superior human beings having great height and four legs as well as two heads. If you do not have a frame of reference it is difficult to listen and fully understand. To paraphrase T S Eliot, 'We hear the words but miss the meaning.'

PERSONAL AGENDAS

Sometimes we work to our personal agendas rather than that of the client. If you are convinced that all psychological problems are due to someone's early toilet training, that all men are not to be trusted or women take relationships too seriously, then there is a tendency to push the conversation of the client in the direction you want it to go. In this way you ensure you get the answers you want. A tale was told of an archaeologist who was caught with hammer and chisel enlarging one of the tombs in the pyramids. When challenged he was reported to have said 'But according to my calculations the tomb is too small, I am correcting the error!' What is interesting is that sometimes clients of counsellors from a Freudian school enjoy dreams appropriate to a Freudian interpretation and if they then change to a Jungian counsellor, after a while, so does their dream pattern.

In my own training I can remember presenting my paper in seminars and knowing that as soon as I touched one of my tutor's academic hot buttons he would say 'That is interesting, perhaps we should pause here.' We soon learnt that if you wanted to deliver the bulk of your paper before any discussion, you had to construct the essay to leave his hot topics until last.

All of us have 'hot buttons' and personal agendas but in counselling the trick is to be aware of them, control them and not let them get in the way of the process.

RAPPORT

Rapport skills are essential in counselling. They are the equivalent of the doctor's bedside manner, the diplomat's charm and the salesman's bonhomie. Essentially rapport is a communications bridge, or a conduit, between you and your client. You are separate individuals but can communicate and understand each other over the rapport bridge between you, rather than shouting at each other from the opposite banks. The bridge itself is not the communication, it just facilitates it. It is possible to work without rapport, but it is much easier with it. Machines work better with well-oiled parts and in the words of the song 'It ain't what you do it's the way that you do it'.

Rapport is not part of the counselling process (although some would argue that it was), but it makes what you do more effective and certainly more pleasant.

Whilst rapport is essentially a natural process, what follow are some ideas and skills which you may wish to try or experiment with. As pointed out elsewhere, you would be wise to practise (and make all your mistakes) outside the counselling rooms before you begin to try the techniques with your clients. As with all things, practice helps achieve perfection, so practise with friends and colleagues before going live.

Physical matching
It is a strange fact that people who like each other and who enjoy good rapport physically match each other's

THE BASIC SKILLS OF COUNSELLING

body language and behaviour. It is said that this is a universal phenomenon of rhythmic alignment. Watch people in social gatherings and it is almost like a dance; they move forward and back together, cross their legs at the same time and move their hands together. This is called matching or bio rapport.

If you as the counsellor use the same alignments of your body as your client, then you are saying to him at a subliminal level that you value or prize him and want to be in rapport with him so that you can work together.

Other things can be included here, such as breathing rates and style – not only breathing in and out at the same time, but also breathing lightly or deeply, depending what the client is doing.

Note:
- It is essential that you practise this outside your counselling sessions until you are proficient and you can appear completely natural. If your client thinks you are mimicking them then your counselling relationship will be severely jeopardized. Your matching has to be natural for if it is not, you will offend the important principle of being genuine and having positive regard for your client.
- If your client has an overt, or out of the ordinary body movement such as a 'facial tic' or 'sham' then it would be inappropriate for you to mimic this aspect of your client's behaviour. There are methods of matching such aspects. Forms of language that clients use can also be matched and if you find this aspect interesting then read up on it or put yourself on an NLP programme.
- Please remember this strategy just supports rapport, it is not in itself a therapeutic aid. All the rapport in

the world is not going to move a client our of their difficulty and on to a more satisfactory life.

Use your client's language

We have already spoken of avoiding clinical or professional jargon with your client, but this is slightly different.

We are more likely to accept people who are like ourselves. Experiments in the 60s revealed we were even more likely to trust someone with the same eye colour as ourselves! If it works for eye colour then why not language and speech patterns. Match, where possible, your client's form of speech: speed, tone, inflection. Enter, where possible, their verbal world.[12]

Each of us has verbal idiosyncrasies – words which we use more regularly than others or words to punctuate what we say – 'OK', 'I mean', 'All right'. Teenagers are not the only group in society that have their own 'in-words', adults do as well – 'ongoing', 'proactive', etc. There are also words of approval such as 'yes', 'exactly', 'you're right', 'sweet'.

By listening to a client carefully you can use the same words and speech patterns when appropriate.[13] It will mean far more to the client than it does to you but that is the whole purpose of the exercise.

However, the same proviso operates here as in matching body language – it must appear natural. If you are well into middle age you might appear less than genuine making statements such as 'You beauty, that fazes me the way you have put your shit together'!

[12] O'Hanlon, W H & Wilk, J, *Shifting Contexts*, Guilford (1987)
[13] Tannen, D, *That's not what I meant!* London: Virago (1992)

MAINTAINING THE PROGRESS

Of course counselling is not just sitting down and asking questions and listening to someone, hoping that as they talk to you and through your empathetic encouragement they suddenly discover elegant solutions to their difficulties and a viable therapeutic action plan, and can go off into the sunset to live happily ever after. Would that life and counselling were that simple.

Although empathetic listening is better for the client than no support at all and there is undoubtedly a genuine cathartic effect that results from an emotional outpouring to another, the process requires a little more.

As counsellors we need to achieve a balance between the nebulousness of non-directiveness and the turbo-driven, supercharged drive to achieve successful goals. Clients do expect change or movement and thus there is the assumption of a process which will achieve benefit – moving from a state of pain to a state of ease. It is then a source of development on both sides working with a therapeutic direction and vision. If we are to achieve this we have to be skilled in attending and the like, but also be in control of the process and it is to this aspect of counselling that we now turn.

THE STAGES IN THE PROCESS

Counselling is like building a house or cooking a meal, it is best done in an agreed predetermined sequence. It is not the 'what' but the 'how' – with an emphasis on the process or building blocks that you use. As the Queen told Alice in Wonderland, 'Start at the beginning and go on to the end'.

Clients, too, are keen for structure and want to know

what is going to happen – then when and the how.[14] What follows is very much an idealized 'best' way and is not always possible but where you can, especially if you have little experience, the discipline will be of considerable benefit to both you and your clients.

There are six major parts to the process and we will review them in turn:

PREPARATION
INITIAL SESSION
SUBSEQUENT SESSIONS
BUILDING ON SUCCESS
CONCLUDING THE THERAPY
DOING THE PAPERWORK

PREPARATION

Sometimes this is not always possible, but it will help you significantly if you can make the investment in this area.

Client history
This can either be done on a form or through discussion, but you need to know:

1. How did the client get to you; what was the referral process?
2. Has the client had counselling or therapy before and if so when and what for and what was the outcome?
3. Is the client being counselled by anyone else at this time?

[14] Casement, P, *On Learning from the Patient*, Turnstock (1985)

4. What is the client's state of health? Is he currently on any medication? In the past has he been on continuous medication for a significant time (i.e. four weeks or more)?
5. What is the client's family structure and/or background?
6. What are the client's domestic arrangements?
7. What are the client's support systems, if any (spouse, partner, relations, friends, social situation, charities, etc.)?
8. What are his symptoms – especially those which might indicate suicidal tendencies?

Anticipate success

Being positive has salutary effects as well as facilitating the placebo effect. Being positive is to encourage the therapeutic effect.[15] How would you feel if you went to the dentist and the conversation went something like:

'Well, I don't know . . .'
'It is a pretty difficult situation . . .'
'It is a long time since we've done this procedure . . .'
'We don't often get this problem . . .'
'Gee, this is my first time with this . . .'?

The dentist might be exceptionally competent, experienced and qualified but your expectations would be far from satisfactory, as would your level of confidence.

We all know of the placebo effect in medication, and it is the same in counselling. It is important for you to be

[15] Lambert, N J et al, 'The Effectiveness of Psychotherapy', in S L Garfield & A E Bergin (Eds) *Handbook of Psychotherapy and Behaviour Change (3rd Edition)* (pp 157 ff). Wiley (1986)

confident, calm and to anticipate an acceptable result. Notice that is an *acceptable* result. Unreasonable expectations need to be challenged and despatched.

'No, I cannot guarantee a happy marriage for you, but what we can do is to help you understand your current difficulties and you will be able to develop tips and strategies so that you can argue less with your partner when you are under strain.'

Decide on an Approach
What do you want to do with the client and what approaches are you going to trial? It is not helpful to give labels to clients. It is not helpful to tell the client:

'You are in the early stage of dysthymic disorder and your personality is showing avoidance features with sociopathic implications.'

You need to recognize the problem and record the matter in your notes, but it is much better to zero in on mind-set, behaviour and emotions of your client and why life is currently difficult for them.

Here are some ideas to help you decide.

1. Identify the specifics of success
What would be relief or success from the client's viewpoint? This should be as specific as possible in terms of actual behaviours. Less stressed, less depressed, more happy are not good enough because they are too vague. One man's happiness is another man's depression. You need to get specific answers. If this is difficult for the client, ask them what would they be doing differently for someone who does not know them well to notice a difference in them – how would an old friend who had

not seen you for some time recognize the changes in you?

2. Why now?
What is it that has brought this person to you today? What are the antecedents or changes in their life that have them recognizing that not only do they need help but they need counselling now and with you? Why you?

3. How has the client coped so far?
It is rare for clients to be in a total state of collapse or inertia, the pain has usually been festering and suppurating for some time. So discover what they are doing or have done to help themselves. This will help you construct and develop treatment protocols because you have an indication of what works for them so far and what has not been of value.[16]

4. Agree goals
We have already examined the success criteria but during the initial session, where possible, further work should be done on goals. Here are a few guidelines:

A. Realistic: They must be real and recognized as such by the client. You can reduce a stammer but are unlikely to get an orator; you can reduce the fear of spiders but it is unlikely your client will become an entomologist. After counselling, individuals are going to be essentially the same person only coping better. Like having a haircut you are the same person, perhaps a little tidier but most of your friends won't recognize that you have been to the hairdresser anyway.

[16] de Sharze, S, *Keys to Solutions in Brief Therapy*, Norton (1983)

B. Measurable: Wherever possible make the goals quantifiable so that you and your client can monitor and measure progress and hopefully move forward. If progress cannot be measured then no one will ever know there has been an improvement.

C. Positive: Goals should be phrased positively. 'To be less worried' is not as appropriate as 'to be confident'. Negatives like 'worried', 'depressed', 'anxious' do not have within them positive information. For someone 'not to worry' requires them to remind themselves of what worry is in the first place so they do not have to do it! Very difficult.

D. Controllable: Clients need control over their goals. Do not be tempted to set them for them because it will invite the response 'You told me to do such and such and I didn't think I could do that, but I didn't want to tell you', or 'I did exactly as you told me and it didn't work'.

E. Achievable: Always work in the area of the possible and what can reasonably be achieved by the client. This also applies to the clients themselves, who sometimes overestimate their ability for positive change or become too enthusiastic. Occasionally, clients will give themselves impossible goals – lose ten kilos in a month, find a husband within three weeks, pat the first dog I see, pick up tarantulas – by giving themselves mission impossible they give themselves permission to fail because the goal was too great.

F. Relevant: Goals should be seen as directly relating to the problem that the client wants rectifying.

G. Possible: That is to say that the client's environment

must be such that he or she has the opportunity to practise new behaviours. Opportunity to practise achievement must be available to the client. Sometimes family,
friends or the workplace have a vested interest in keeping the client and the situation at the status quo.

It is helpful if goals are expressed in a positive way. Thus
'I want to be more assertive, relaxed, in control' etc, is
far superior to 'I want to be less mild, anxious or confused.'
   The use of questions can be very helpful here.

'What is it that you would like?'
'Can you tell me why that is important for you?'
'Is that your wish or has someone else suggested that it
might be a good idea for you?'
'What are the main three or four reasons why this is
important for you?'
'What will be the benefits that achievement will bring?'
'What will be the milestones along the way to success?'

Goals are like political agendas – they change over time
and the client has the control over what they wish to
deal with. Just like a patient who goes to the doctor with
a hamstring injury and then develops pneumonia, it
would be a strange physician who insisted on dealing
with the hamstring first.
   Pain and problems that clients present are usually
symptomatic of more significant or bigger problems and
often as a counsellor you will be tempted to move on to
the large issues whilst the client is content with the quick
solution. Being unable to talk to men may be the problem because of child abuse, but the client may not wish
to deal with that issue once she has been able to go to
parties, dancing and go out on dates. Unless the client is

likely to endanger himself or others in the goals he pursues, then the role of the counsellor is to follow rather than lead, to go no further than the client wants to go.

5. Agree reward systems

This comes straight from classical behaviourism as identified by Pavlov and Skinner. How is the client going to be rewarded when behaviour moves in the appropriate direction? Since you as the counsellor will not be there the client can perform this task. Client and counsellor agree together what would constitute a positive reward and what would constitute a 'gentle' punishment. (See page 52/53). It is important to note that punishment is not for 'failure' but for 'not trying'. Most of our work is to encourage clients to have the courage to try, and with any new behaviour early failure goes with the territory. The last thing we want is to punish someone for trying!

The reward should be something meaningful and valued by the client and similarly the punishment a personal 'hate'. Interestingly, but not surprisingly, one client's reward is another client's punishment!! Rewards are to be taken as soon after the goal or standard set has been achieved and punishment is to be endured as soon after the event of 'not trying'.

Clients are to remind themselves why they are rewarding or punishing themselves and reflect on what they could do when the next opportunity occurs.

EXAMPLES OF REWARDS AND PUNISHMENTS

Tea	Going without tea
Coffee	Going without coffee
Ice-cream	Going without sugar
Cigarettes	Missing a meal

A walk	Being grounded
Company of a friend	Not seeing friends
Food	Eating something healthy you don't like
A snack	No TV or favourite programme
A book	No newspaper
Meal out	Early to bed
Shopping	Early to rise
A purchase	Fasting
Sweets	Cleaning shoes
Newspaper	Ironing
TV	Cooking
Video	Washing paintwork
Make-up	Scrubbing the floor
Sports fixture	Washing the car
Clothes	No golf
An early night	No gardening
Sex	Have cold foods for a day
Cinema	Wear something you don't like
A night out	Walking a mile to work
A night in	Writing a letter
An outing	Push-ups
A telephone chat	Giving money away
Exercise	Cleaning the car
A visit to a friend	Staying late at work
A social event	No social telephoning
Time for a holiday	Drinking only water
Shower/bath	

THE INITIAL SESSION

1. Show the client you care, demonstrate empathy
Get into rapport with your client and stay there. You

only get one chance at making a first impression and it should be positive. Clients will often make an instant decision about you based not on your competence, your qualifications or your reputation but how they feel about you after the first five minutes of contact.

A useful strategy here is to keep finding things in the client that you like, admire or can respect. This will often initiate an improving spiral of mutual regard.[17]

2. Understand what the client wants

What is it specifically the client wants and expects? Discover the 'pain' that brought them to you. This will give you an opportunity early on to formulate some possible initial approaches and also to contract with the client. (See page on Contracting.)

See if you can't encapsulate in as few sentences as possible exactly what the client's problem is and their success criteria are, for example:

'Your boss makes you feel inadequate in your professional knowledge and you would like her to work with you as a colleague?'

'Your wife has had an affair and you want help to decide what the best options are for you within the marriage?'

'You have been fired from your job and you want to explore what you might be successful at if you did something completely different?'

'Because your last boyfriend beat you up badly you have fears about going into a relationship with another

[17] Aranson, E, *The Social Animal* (6th Edition), Freeman (1992)

man and you do not want to make the same mistake again?'

It is useful to put the summary as a question then the client feels able to confirm or expand further their difficulties. Not all the initial problems are the 'real' problem.

3. Talk about the process
What is going to happen? What are the options for the client, how long will the sessions be, how many sessions initially, what will be the fee structure, if any, and what outcomes could reasonably be expected?

THE APPROACH

If you are not a trained therapist then it is unlikely that you will be working over long periods with your clients and, although the skills for long or short periods of therapy have much in common, the process and the constraints you will probably be working to are likely to be more focused or condensed. Simply because you have less time, you are in crisis mode or just the person who happens to be there when the emotional dam breaks.

Even if you are just acting like a paramedic, being the first on the scene before the professionals can take over from you it is important to manage the approach appropriately. Here are some of the main components and concepts for you with which you can work.

Use of time
Prevent yourself or the client from wasting the time available to you both. Use every moment productively and if a session 'is over' don't feel obliged to keep it

going unnecessarily. Use time flexibly and creatively – not everyone needs to see you once a week, not everyone needs exactly 50 minutes.

Work to goals

Goals are helpful to both counsellor and client, for you it gives direction and for the client a sense of well-being, so work towards what the client wants as soon as possible.[18]

Negotiate and agree goals with the client so that both of you know and are totally committed to what you want and what is possible. Research has shown that objectives which are behaviourally defined help clients become optimistic about outcomes. (See the section on Goals on page 51ff.) More importantly, quantified goals will help the client recognize success, however small, when it is achieved.

This may sound very clinical and impersonal but it is essential to the process and you can still show genuine concern for the individual. Do not be over-vigorous. It is obvious, for example, that when someone has just been told they have terminal cancer, asking what their goals are is not an appropriate intervention.

Sometimes clients are so confused or anxious that they have no idea what is wrong or how to express their difficulties. They just 'feel down' and 'everything is on top of them' and they 'can't cope anymore'. Discussion here about goals is also inappropriate. What they want is to 'feel good' and 'to be on top of things' and 'able to cope', which are far too nebulous to work on but through non-directive discussion an agenda will slowly manifest itself.

[18] Csikszentmihalyi, M, *Flow: The Psychology of Optional Experience*, Harper Perennial (1990)

In working around this subject it is important to differentiate between:

Wishes – things which would be nice
Aims   – things which are hoped for
Goals – things for which there is some real commitment

Sometimes it is helpful to work through with the client a process of MILD which stands for:

Must have   It is very important that the client achieves this and he is prepared to put effort and personal sacrifice into achieving this goal. For him this is the bottom line.

Intend to have   What the client hopes to gain and will work towards, but not be too surprised or disappointed if he doesn't achieve it.

Like to have   This is the area of fantasy. If clients could change themselves and their world, what would they want?

Don't want   Just as there are secondary benefits in change, so there are secondary disadvantages. What does the client definitely want to avoid, either in his present state or in the future when the change is wrought?

Total focus and rank order difficulties

It is not possible to work on all the problems all the time, so rank order them. Negotiate with the client which one they are to resolve first, second, third, etc. and then proceed to work in that order unless the client wants to change it.[19] Keep the client focused and working on what you have agreed. Sometimes the client will want to 'get off the hook' by moving too quickly down the list; sometimes you will feel more comfortable working with something else, but avoid the temptation. Some have called this the *salami technique*. You never eat all the salami all at once but in very thin slices. Have counselling slices until the whole length of the problem is sliced away, then on to the next salami.

What usually happens is that in dealing with the client's main concerns the minor issues just fall away anyway, but the converse is not true. If you start with the insignificant problems (going for an early kill) the real problems become more difficult.

Stay in the 'now'

Of course every problem has an ontology or a history and of course 'why' the problem has arisen is also important, especially for some clients, but what people want is 'relief now'. The past is only relevant in that it helps you understand the present so that something can be done about the future. Essentially 'knowing why' is not as important in terms of relief as 'doing something now'. You will find that many clients, once they have relief from their immediate problem, no longer need to see you because they can now manage to resolve and work through the subsidiary problems.

Leave the 'why' to the professional therapists who are trained in resolving causes as well as relieving symptoms. When you go to your dentist in pain you want relief now rather than a long explanation as to the inadequacies of your personal oral hygiene schedules over

[19] Blackburn, I M, and Davidson, K, *Cognitive Therapy for Depression and Anxiety*, Oxford: Blackwell (1990)

the past two years! Relieve the pain then deal, if necessary, with the causes. Certainly people in crisis want symptom relief.

Staying on the rock

Giving total focus and staying in the 'now' can be illustrated by the figure below:

	Now	Today	Tomorrow	Next Week	Next Month	Next Year	Some Time
Myself	ROCK						
My family		SAND					
My friends							
Colleagues					SWAMP		
Community							
Society							

In working with your client continually ask yourself 'where are we in this discussion?'. If you are not dealing with the client directly and the time is not imminent then it is highly likely that the focus and staying 'in the now' has slipped and needs to be recaptured. Some clients are brilliant at keeping themselves and you in the swamp with the length of the discussion the inverse of progress.

Give permission for emotions

Problems where people seek counselling are usually more to do with heart and tummy than the head. People *feel* their pain, anguish and anxiety. Clients feel 'gutted' rather than 'brain dead'. Expressions of feelings bring relief and are cathartic in their own right. Expressions of anger, fear and frustration have their place in the therapeutic process and are to be recognized if not actively encouraged, especially in the initial stages or when the 'real' problem surfaces.

Your job is to provide a safe environment where emotions can be displayed and to show that such behaviour is 'OK'. This relates directly back to the section on empathy. Tears are the balm of the tormented and laughter the gateway to happiness.

Do what works – be eclectic
The blessing and the curse of counselling is that there is no single way of helping clients manage their difficulties. There are many schools of thought and different types of therapies, each bringing practical help in certain situations, with certain types of clients at certain times. All these variables mean that you have to stay flexible in your approach. 'If what you are doing is not working, do something different' is not only a good maxim for therapy, it is also good as a life rule. The more you understand about different techniques the more able you will be to customize your work to the special needs of your client.[20] If you follow just one technique you will be severely limited. Remember that to a hammer every screw is just a badly finished nail! You need more than hammers and screwdrivers in your tool-box.

STRATEGIES, TACTICS AND TIPS

In this section we examine some of the ways to help clients change their behaviour and move towards their goals. Because of the many variables in the situations, it is not possible to advise when to use which or which is

[20] Howard, J et al, *Adaptive Counselling and Therapy*, Jossey-Bass (1987)

best in what situation. Also, because of your disposition and experience you will be more drawn to some suggestions than others. What is important is to move through the suggestions efficiently and quickly until you discover what works for you in your situation with your clients, and how comfortable you feel deploying them.

Please regard this section as a set of cards with some being trump cards in some games but not in others. You also have to be flexible and creative in your use of your cards – don't gamble at the client's expense. Nor is what follows a complete deck – new cards are being discovered all the time and some are used just once and never played again.

All interventions, of course, are made with the best of intentions with the client's welfare paramount not their manipulation.

Skills and techniques of therapy need not be confined to the counselling session and it is recommended that you practice those card games which are new to you on friends and colleagues to gain proficiency first. As you gain confidence then slowly play them into your sessions and make notes on the outcomes and successes that you achieve with them. Note down failures, too.

The order of the suggestions made here are to be taken as indicating importance – all can make a significant contribution in their own right. Nor does their position indicate the skill level required to use them effectively.

1. Use your client's frames of reference and interests
Most people put effort and hard work into something in their lives.[21] Sometimes it is a hobby or a sport, a leisure

---

[21] Omer, H, 'Enhancing the Impact of Therapeutic Interventions', *Ann. J. Of Psychotherapy* (1992) 44 (2) 218 ff

activity like reading or watching videos, or a belief system like church or charity work. Many clients give much of their disposable time and income to these.

The more you can live in the client's world, accept their concepts and ideas, irrespective of how strange they are, the easier it is to direct them.[22]

It is very rare you find someone who is not motivated or does not get excited about something and this area provides a rich vein for therapeutic stories, analogies and metaphors. The proximity of the consultant to the client's experience and belief system is directly proportional to your therapeutic influence.

For example, an executive was referred to me – he was over-stressed and working far longer than necessary. His excessive hours were not thought to be necessary by his superiors and morale was down and turnover up because he expected the same of his staff. He was working hard but not smart. The highlight of this man's week was his squash game on Sunday mornings with his friends. We had discussions around sport and how interesting it was that a game of squash was 40 minutes and yet a game of soccer 90 minutes. I wondered what would happen if he played squash for 90 minutes. Injury and exhaustion came the quick reply. I then went on to wonder what would happen if someone worked 80 hours a week instead of the 45 most executives worked. He was to think about that and let me know at our next session. The answer and the resultant behaviour were predictable.

2. Use the client's beliefs about themselves
If someone has irrational beliefs and he has invested a significant part of his life constructing these belief

[22] Erickson, M and Rossi, E, *Experiencing Hypnosis* Irvington (1981)

systems it is very difficult to meet them head on and attempt to change them. Belief systems are like our 'comfortable blankets' and bring tremendous relief; they are almost our psychological shield to fend off the vicious vicissitudes that would make victims of us.

A very young person was referred to me because she thought she was dyslexic. Her earlier scholastic performance indicated that she was normal but somehow for the past two years she had refused to read 'because she could not, being so severely dyslexic'. During a session we set up a project for her of discovering famous dyslexics – I already knew that many were famous actors and actresses and we reviewed them when she brought her list back. We then discussed how these famous dyslexic people became so good at acting and learning lines. They had to read them again and again and it was suggested she learn, like famous dyslexics, speeches from the more popular Shakespearean plays *Romeo and Juliet* and *A Midsummer Night's Dream*. First by listening to her parents, then from tapes, but she was to follow the script. It was engineered that gradually the voices on the tapes spoke more slowly, her parents stumbled over words and it wasn't long before our young client was correcting them or wanting to read faster. From plays we moved to historical or cultural background reading because this is how the actresses became so good and it was not long before she was reading again. She also went on to star in the school play.

3. Binds
Binds give the client the illusion of choice. Ownership and control are important for clients; many attend counselling because they feel they lack confidence or there is little in their lives that they control. Binds are useful in this respect.

Essentially a bind is a sophisticated either/or. Either you do this or you do that, with both 'this' and 'that' being what you want the client to attempt. Rather like the sales assistant who says 'How are you going to pay? Cash or credit card?' – whichever way you answer you end up paying!

Here are some examples:

'Which part of your background do you want to work on first?'

The underlying assumption here is that the client is going to work on his or her background and which part is worked on first is of little significance.

Similarly,

'Would you like to work in that chair or should we move to something more comfortable?'

Binds can also be presumptive thereby anticipating something happening,

'Before we deal with your specific difficulty let me tell you how I like to work.'

Or, more sophisticated,

'For the really best results it is important that you don't work too quickly through this.'

It is elegant because it presumes the best results will be achieved and encourages the client to work thoroughly through the process at whichever speed the counsellor feels is appropriate – how is the client likely to know what 'too quickly' means! But he or she knows they are going to get 'best results'.

4. Implications
This is bringing to the client anything which recognizes, encourages or rewards the client's efforts.

'I don't know whether or not you have noticed but since you have been coming here/working more/thinking about/etc, etc, such and such has happened.'

or

'You probably haven't noticed, but since you have . . . such and such has happened.'

The first observation has to be verifiable by the client for the second half to be accepted.

'You will be interested to know that since you have been thinking about your future I feel your decision-making ability has really improved.'

And here is a bind for you the reader . . .

'Now that you have got this far in the book and we are reviewing counselling techniques, I wonder if you have noticed how much more flexible you are becoming.'

Nothing breeds success, so we are told, like success. It is good for clients to feel their efforts are recognized, no matter how small. (See section on Rewarding and Congratulating clients.)

The 'I feel' in the penultimate statement makes it less open to debate or question by the client. It is difficult to challenge how someone feels. If you say 'I think you are . . .' then the client can go on into a denial-debate mode.

Examples of binds – illusion of alternatives
Simple
1. Which part of your relationship with your partner do you want to work on first?
2. Shall we look at your strengths or weaknesses?
3. Would you prefer to work at a desk or should we move to something more comfortable?
4. Which difficulty do you think it would be most profitable to review first?

Binds of Presumption
1. Before we get direction on your career, let me explain the process.
2. It is important that you don't work too quickly on this.
3. When you work on your affirmations you can really use your imagination.
4. Have you worked on your career **before**?

Presumption After
1. How was that?
2. How does this work compare to what you did before?

Binds of Implication
1. I don't know whether you noticed but since . . . such and such has happened.
2. You probably are not aware, but since . . . such and such has happened.

5. Role play
One way of providing a link between the counselling

session and the real world is by use of role play. As the counsellor you can be the object of the client's fear, anger, anxiety and let them act out the issues they wish. These can be in the past, such as hurtful conversations with significant others or imaginary conversations they wished they had had with significant others.

If you wish to observe, then a variant would be to suggest to the client they address themselves to an empty chair. Should you think of employing this strategy you may wish to try it on your own first so that you can share the experience.

Future projections and rehearsals can also be role-played. 'Supposing I was your husband/boss/lover/friend, what would you want to say to me if you wanted to . . .', 'What other ways could you say that?', 'Which do you think would be most appropriate?', 'Would you like to practise it again, making what you say as realistic as possible?'. Although this is role play, be yourself as much as possible.

Closely associated with role play is role reversal. That is playing the role of the antagonist. The purpose here is to help the client understand and begin to experience what the other person thinks and feels. It is an ideal way of reducing self-referencing by clients.

Role plays are not for everyone, some people lack the imagination or the creativity to make it work or have difficulty expressing feelings and emotions. Role plays, whilst useful, are not real life; they are artificial and clients can come back to a counselling session disappointed that the real thing did not follow the predetermined script of the role play. Finally, what people do in role plays and what they do in life are sometimes completely different. However, for all these difficulties role plays are useful in experiencing, planning for and undertaking changes in interpersonal behaviour.

6. Deframing and Reframing

Clients report facts and the meanings they have added to them, i.e. their own interpretations to those facts. You can challenge those facts and this is called *deframing*, or you can work with the client to develop a new set of meanings, which help him accept the situation. If a new set of meanings is accepted by the client then this is *reframing*.

Changing the way the client thinks and interprets facts can either make the client more open to a therapeutic intervention or indeed resolve the whole 'problem'. Thus, for example, a difficult child, rather than being a burden and a trial to a mother, can be an opportunity to show her motherly love. A personal example is that as a young man I became concerned that I was losing my hair, until I was told that men high in testosterone usually suffered hair loss. I doubt whether this is true, but to an 18-year-old this macho myth, I remember, was a great comfort until I realized that for most relationships hair was not a critical issue. Reframes help ugly duckling clients think of themselves as swans. In life, bottles which are half empty are also half full.

In most weaknesses there is a strength to be identified and there is usually a gift in every problem that besets us.

A fact is what has happened; a story is the gloss that is put on the facts. It is very difficult for individuals to separate the two components and it is usually the latter that inflicts the pain. As a counsellor you can do your client a great service by encouraging them to be skilled in splitting or putting a wedge between the reality and its interpretation.

Here are some examples:

My husband is angry with me ∴ I'm neglected

My wife withholds sex	∴	I'm repulsive
I made a mistake	∴	I'm incompetent
My boss bullies me	∴	I'm a wimp

As you can see, the interpretation is unreasonable based upon such limited reality. By gently challenging clients about what are the facts and what is their story it is possible for them to

1. Develop another set of reasons explaining the behaviour of others which then makes their story about themselves inappropriate.

and/or

2. Make possible a reframe band, thus creating another story which fits the facts but is not so debilitating.

For example, my husband is angry with me. He could be angry because:

1. He is in pain
2. He can't be angry at work
3. He is frustrated with himself
4. He has a behavioural problem
5. He is covering for some fault he has

Reframes could be:

1. You are only angry with people you love – if you don't feel for them why bother?
2. He thinks you are strong enough to take it.
3. You're the only one he feels safe enough with to express his emotions.
4. He wants to test your love for him.

71

5. It is his way of expressing his masculinity.

7. Work on a different problem

Success is contagious and working on a different problem can frequently help the main difficulty. So, for example, a man who has difficulty relating to the opposite sex could be encouraged to take up tap dancing or learn a foreign language. In both these activities there are likely to be far more women than men and he will thus increase his contact with women. A woman who feared men physically could be encouraged to take up karate or car maintenance. She would come into contact with far more men than women and learn that only a small percentage of men fit into her categorization of them. A woman who once had a fear of dogs was encouraged to work with blind people. She soon learnt how beneficial dogs could be.

8. Permission to fail

What does a baby that has just learnt to walk do when it wants to get from A to B? It reverts to crawling, which it knows it can do more effectively than walking. To learn to walk requires falling regularly. According to some scientists we fail in our attempts to walk no less than 1,500 times! As a counsellor you can use this likelihood of failure in a positive manner by giving clients permission to fail. For example:

'This is quite complicated. Most people can't do it when they try for the first three or four attempts, but by the fifth attempt it just comes.'

or

'You will really be surprised, it is so difficult to do on the

72

first two or three occasions and then suddenly you are just doing it.'

When the client attempts the new behaviour he fails. The counsellor predicted this and since he was right the credibility of the permission to fail statement is increased. Similar subsequent attempts also fail, but because the client expects to be successful the predicted attempt achieves just that! As Henry Ford said elsewhere, 'If you think you can or you can't, you're right.'

9. Assumptive language

This technique comes from sales rather than therapy but is nevertheless useful. It assumes success or a behaviour will occur. A car salesman might say 'When you drive this new car you will find . . .' In counselling this can translate to:

'When you do . . . you will find that . . .'

As you can see it is assumed from the outset that the client will take action as required – non-compliance is not an issue. It is not 'If you . . .' but 'When you . . .' You can also use 'As you . . .'

'As you go through therapy you will find . . .'

You can even add a 'band-wagon' effect – clients feel safety in numbers.

'As you go through therapy, like everyone else, you will . . .'

'What has improved since last time?'

Obviously what is neat in this last statement is that improvement is assumed. Clients, for obvious reasons, come to sessions concentrating on their difficulties. This assumptive technique goes a long way to redress the balance.

In my group sessions I used the following set of questions which participants either answer individually and receive comment from the rest of the group, or the whole group addresses:

1. 'What have you done since we last met?'
2. 'What worked?'
3. 'What did you find interesting?'
4. 'What will you do differently next time?'
5. 'What would you like to discuss?'

Questions 3 and 4 are interesting. It invites negativity if you ask 'What went wrong?' or 'What didn't work?'. But the learning and development aspects of what went wrong are encapsulated in 'What was interesting?' or 'What would you do differently?'. If what the client achieved was successful and brought them nearer their goal they are unlikely to want to do it differently in the future.

10. Past coping behaviour

Clients develop their own coping behaviour to give themselves relief. Sometimes this behaviour is aberrant and inappropriate but occasionally they discover ways of coping which you as the counsellor can incorporate into your treatment schedule. Even the aberrant behaviour can be amended to bring about the results in the appropriate direction.

11. Milestones

It is unlikely that anyone can get perfection immediately,

as in graph *i*. Development and growth in human behaviour is not a step function, but rather gradual increments of learning with brief plateaux of consolidation, as in graph *ii*.

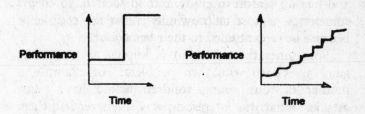

i. STEP FUNCTION   *ii INCREMENTS WITH PLATEAUX*

At each plateau try to set up a milestone of achievement. It might not be the ideal result but it is a point of achievement which needs recognition. Facing a large change can be daunting but making several small achievements is highly motivating and encouraging.

Take advantage too of encouraging the client to look back to see what he has achieved. Rather like climbing a mountain – you might not be at the top but to look back and view where you have come from is most satisfying.

'What can you do now that you could not do when we started working together?'

'What can you do now that you could not do when you first had this difficulty?'

Milestones are also occasions for rewards and celebrations.

12. Use resistance and challenges

Clients put a lot of effort into their behaviour patterns and even when they come to you for help, sometimes they want to hang on to their old behaviour.[23] It is comfortable for them. Rather like a dog that has lost its fleas and has no reason to enjoy a good scratch, so clients sometimes, almost unknowingly, resist the counsellor because he is so attuned to their behaviour.

Sometimes there is what is known as 'secondary gain' associated with their problem. For example, a mother of four young children would have panic attacks. What was interesting was she never had them when she was on her own with her children, but only in the presence of other adults, especially her husband. The secondary gain here was that the attack provided the woman with the secondary gains of:

1. Respite from childminding duties
2. Sympathy from the adult that was present, especially her husband.

If her difficulty brought these advantages it is not surprising that she was initially somewhat resistant to constructive therapy.

Another approach is to go with the resistance and let it be the client's problem. By allowing or recognizing the resistance the client then has to fight to justify himself to himself rather than to another person. For example:

'You seem to have done so well and you cope OK, why do you want assistance from me?'

'Your family don't seem to mind all that much, why

[23] Ascher, L M (Ed), *Therapeutic Paradox*, Guilford (1989)

does it concern you?'

'But your shouting at your daughter makes her behave in the way you want, so why are you trying to change the relationship?'

'Being quiet and non-assertive makes you popular with most people, why change?'

If the client challenges you after such statements they also confront and challenge themselves.

13. Challenge the perceptions

This is best explained by an example. A young man was referred to me because he kept being dismissed from work as he kept breaking the rules. In our sessions he said he hated rules, was incapable of keeping them because he was a 'rule-breaker'. It also transpired that he played football, which was the great love of his life, and it was easy to challenge him as to why it was he could play football with all its rules and regulations.

He went on to become a football referee.

Little challenges help. For example:

'I'm confused here. Why is it you can control your temper with your male boss but not your husband, and yet you have said that both of them annoy you?'

There are five major areas of challenge.[24]

1. Information – are the facts correct?
2. Client's concerns

[24] Swain, J, *The Use of Counselling Skills*, Butterworth-Heinemann, (1995)

3. Relationships
4. Client self-awareness
5. Counsellor self-awareness

This then leads to opportunities to generalize the coping behaviour to situations when there is a problem.

Another variation of a challenge is to enquire what would happen in the medium term if they did not change and whether it would really have any significant consequence anyway. Rather like trying to make a decision, when you write down the positives and negatives associated with each – have the client do the same.

Challenges are not popular with counsellors for in some way they go against the interpersonal requirements demanded by both rapport and the process. Clients, however, are usually stronger than we give them credit. As experience develops you will just know when it is appropriate and when it is not. But in any case it should be part of your skill portfolio for the benefits of challenging are legion.[25]

14. Changing established patterns

This is almost the *salami technique* we have mentioned before. Take the problem a slice at a time. Rome was not built in a day, nor are you likely to change your client overnight. Just establish a small change in their behaviour each time you meet. If your client can get some control over even the smallest aspect of the undesired experience or behaviour which they have recognized and accepted – this is progress. It is rather like a small crack in the dam. The resistance is significantly reduced and eventually will erode the whole structure.

To do this is very important to discover *when* and

[25] Davanloo, H, *Unlocking the Unconscious*, Wiley (1990)

how the problem is manifested. What day, what time of day, with whom, where, what leads up or goes before the onset of the undesired event or behaviour. You are looking for clues. How does it occur, what do they do? Get as much specific behaviour as possible. How frequently does it happen, what sort of intensity, who is there?

Once the facts have been discovered then introduce variations to break the habit or the environmental factors that prompt it. For example, smokers will have a chair in which they usually have a cigarette or a specific time, say after a meal, when they 'habitually' indulge. Get them to use a different chair or engage immediately in washing-up before sitting down; anything that breaks the habit in some way.

There are many ways of effecting changes in behaviour patterns:

Change the place
Change the time
Change the actors
Change the frequency
Change the sequence of events
Interrupt the sequence
Increase the intensity
Decrease the intensity
Miss out parts of the sequence
Reverse the sequence

Here are some examples of changing established patterns:

A mother referred her son because he was always daydreaming and this was thought to be having an adverse effect on his school work. We established special 'dream times' that he would reward himself with if he paid attention during the important subjects at school, such as English and Maths. Later, dream times were speeded up and then moved to more appropriate times outside the classroom.

A woman who was overweight could eat anything she wished whenever she wished providing she ate spinach, which she hated, before she snacked.

A woman suffered from flatulence every time she went dancing, which she loved. She was told to practise breaking wind as she got ready to go out and also after she had been dancing. She learnt control.

A man could only achieve an erection after putting on his Wellington boots. He had to wear his Wellington boots as soon as he got home from work and all during the weekends.

PART 3

Helping with grieving and loss

Most of us when we are grieving for the loss of someone or something move through a recognizable and similar process. Of course there are individual differences because each of us is unique and no two situations are the same, so there are personal variations as to the quality and quantity of the trauma of loss. Those individuals with strong support systems of family and friends and who are well integrated are able to take loss in their stride more easily; however for some it is a very significant psychological event that leaves emotional scars that last a lifetime.

Here are the more familiar 'stages', but remember that not everyone goes through them all and for those that do go through some or any of them it will not necessarily be in the exact order presented here.

The stage of denial: 'I just don't believe this!'
Loss is something that happens to other people and not to us; loss is a part of life and yet we are never quite prepared for it. Most of us live what is sometimes called a rescue fantasy – bad things don't happen to us and if they did someone would somehow rescue us from our pain or difficulty. As humans we hope against hope and

fight off the inevitable by our plans, dreams and fantasies which are then shattered by the stark reality of death, loss and/or the destruction of what is significant to us. Or else we find we are unable either to either heal ourselves or mend significant relationships.

When we come face to face with loss the reality is far too much for us: we cannot cope with the inevitability of what has happened and so we refuse to believe it.

'This can't be' or 'No, you must be wrong' are common reactions. I can remember having to break the news to a teenager that her father, who had been terminally ill for some time, had died while she was taking exams at school. Her response to the news was 'No you are wrong – my dad promised he would be with us at Christmas'.

Consciously or unconsciously we cannot accept the reality and the greater the emotional significance to the individual, the greater the possibility of denial.

The stage of emotional outburst: *'This is just not fair!'*
Once the reality sinks in there is usually some form of emotional response, most commonly anger. This is not always easy for you the counsellor to manage. Angry people are not nice to be around, especially if they are physically powerful and have a history of violence. Sometimes it is turned inwards – 'I did not know that I had this much hate inside me.' Strangely enough the emotional response can sometimes be manic in that the individual laughs or giggles uncontrollably as his way of coping.

The stage of guilt: *'If only I had . . .'*
Humans look for explanations and for causes and where the loss lacks a rational explanation we often create one that imputes guilt to ourselves. 'If only I had looked

after him better.' 'If only I had insisted that she give up smoking twenty years ago.'

Interestingly too, in Western society one is supposed to feel grief at the death of someone but supposing you don't? The response here commonly is guilt. It is often not the case that the person is glad that the individual has died but a sense of relief that they have been released from their pain and suffering. The lack of grief that induces guilt in these circumstances is clearly misplaced.

Sometimes there is guilt because of unfinished conversations or harsh words said in anger or frustration, and the opportunity to put things right is denied through the sudden or unexpected death of the person.

The stage of fantasy: *'If I do such and such perhaps it won't happen'*

People bargain with themselves – or with God – promising to change or be good or to undertake some trial or tribulation so that the situation can be reversed or postponed.

Sometimes the fantasy is rather like denial in that the loss is trivialized or thought not to be significant. Fired executives fantasize about headhunters ringing them up with offers of fabulous jobs, children fantasize that their parents are not divorcing and they will all go on holiday together soon. A husband who has just lost his wife in an affair fantasizes about her coming back to him full of remorse. Of course dreams sometimes come true, but that is usually on celluloid from Hollywood.

> I will be OK
> This is no big deal
> Just watch me bounce back
> She'll be right back
> No problem

Sometimes the fantasy takes the form of bargaining with self, with God or with the therapeutic team. Religious people promise to be good or fulfil religious obligations if only they can hang on for a little longer. Even people without a prior history of faith will turn to the Almighty and effect imaginary bargains for more time. Occasionally it is an indication of unfinished business; the individual has a relationship with someone that needs to be put right before death denies them the opportunity.

With the loss of a loved one fantasy can occur in the form of hallucination, the person affected being usually the wife, partner or friend of long standing. The deceased person is felt to be around, or heard moving about the house or calling out their name. Some people will even see their deceased loved one or find themselves in conversation with them and in rare cases experience being touched by them.

In my experience those who have these hallucinations actually find them comforting but they have the discomfort – because they know on reflection that they are not real – of thinking they are abnormal in some way or showing signs of madness. This phenomenon is too common for this to be so. It is rather the mysteries of the unconscious working, making certain sensations, interpreted in a different way so the person experiences what he dearly wishes for and has lost. In older people it is not uncommon for such experiences to go on ten years or so after the death of their beloved.

The stage of helplessness: '*I just can't cope with this*'
Once you realize that life is not fair, that you too can be one of life's victims and that fantasy offers no more protection – then feelings of helplessness can be quite overwhelming.

Children fear that their other parent is going to die, redundant executives feel they will never work again, the terminally ill feel this dreadfully when it is finally realized that there is no hope of recovery. People who have been beaten, those who have been in serious accidents or seen atrocities committed are convinced that it will happen again and there is nothing they can do.

We seek for reasons why such ills should befall us. An innate sense of justice suggests that something must have happened or been done to bring about this horrendous state of affairs. It is difficult to accept that it is not a fair or just world and that evil does exist, so we cope with it by saying 'What have I done to deserve this?' or in days gone by, 'I am being punished for the sins of my parents'. Sometimes there is self-blame: if only I had done this or that – it is all my fault.

Children become convinced that they are the cause of their parents' break up, survivors of car accidents are convinced even when they were not driving that they were in some way responsible for the accident. This way of thinking preserves our conviction that everything is orderly and that only the bad have bad things happening to them.

> This is just too much
> Nothing can be done
> I always fail/lose/do badly
> I'm always unlucky

The reaction of depression: '*I just don't want to go on any more*'
The intensity of the grief and the sadness match the significance of the loss. People do die of broken hearts. To feel depressed and deeply sad is not a sign of mental instability. It means that feeling and sleeping are difficult

and the company of others is just not welcome. People want to withdraw and weep.

> I'm finished
> No one wants me
> No one loves me
> I'm so alone
> There is no point in anything
> It's not worth it
> I give up

Reaction of acceptance '*I can cope with this*'
Gradually the individual comes to recognize the new situation and begins to marshal resources to meet the problem and grow through it. The loss itself gets into a manageable perspective rather than being suppressed or forgotten altogether. Not infrequently the person in some ways becomes stronger in spite of ordeal and loss. Not that they would wish to go through it again, or indeed wish it upon another, but through it they have discovered more about themselves, their strengths, their resolve, and often claim to be more human.

'In the midst of winter, I have finally discovered that there is within me an inevitable summer.'
  Albert Camus

RAPE

Rape is horrendous because it strikes at the very being of an individual. Not only are the victims physically abused but put in fear of their life – most fear that they will be murdered during or immediately after the event. In rape the individual is totally degraded as a human being and used as the object of the hedonistic will of another who usually uses physical superiority or intimidation to bring about submission. Most rape victims report a state of frozen fright, in as much as they know what is happening but are unable because of their desolate state of terror to be able to defend themselves. Subsequently there are feelings of tremendous self-revulsion and/or guilt, because victims feel that their fear encouraged them into conscious co-operation with the perpetrator. 'I should have done more to defend myself' or 'I can't understand why I gave in so easily' are both common post-event statements.

My view is that this frozen fear is more than just a survival strategy (because if you fought back the violence would escalate) but rather a splitting off of the self from the act – it is occurring but the individual is removing herself psychologically from the event. In a very important way the victim is no longer present.

Rape, then, is far more than physical harm and although that alone is bad enough to induce trauma it is essential to use exceptional empathy in such cases, without a hint of any recrimination against the victim.

Denial is a common initial response to rape and explains why so many cases are not reported. Your case at law is somewhat weakened if the matter is not reported immediately. 'Rape', 'assault', and 'buggery' are very emotionally charged terms and should not be used by the counsellor unless the victim mentions them first. In any event it is the psychological aspect that should be your primary concern, leaving the physical side to the medics.

What is paramount for victims is to regain their self-esteem which has been devastated. Their very being has been brutalized and needs to be nursed back slowly with care and with patience.

Non-directive skills are of the essence here, for the last thing the victim can probably cope with is anything that resembles an interrogation. Open questions are very much the order of the day:

'How do you feel about staying on your own?'

'Whenever you are ready – and there is no rush or urgency – please feel free to talk about what happened.'

Once the victim begins to talk about the event it is not uncommon for her to want to go over and over her recollection. This helps her understand what happened, and to search for an explanation as to why it happened to her and what part she played herself. As she recounts the event the counsellor can be of tremendous help just by encouraging the person to verbalize, recalling as much detail as possible. Through continual re-examination the client slowly comes to the realization that she is truly a victim and that there are vicious people in this world who are closer to their animal instincts than to their humanity. Examples of open questions could be:

'What assistance do you need to help you through this?'

'How would you like me to help – if at all – in talking to your family?'

'What are your feelings about getting some professional counselling support to help you through the next few weeks?'

THREATS OF SUICIDE

These should always be taken seriously. Many actual suicides are suicide gestures or cries for help that go very wrong. Always act on the cry for help, however insignificant you feel the cause of the threat is. We are dealing with clients who are in pain and their perceptions which are not necessarily close to everyday reality. In the majority of cases an actual suicide is the result of a temporary mental aberration or instability – the person is just off balance rather than insane. An anxious event or something quite small pushes the person beyond his limits of personal normal functioning and control. There are social pressures too, that increase the likelihood of suicide: for instance in the US suicide is now the third most common form of death in teenage males, and figures in the UK tend to suggest that this trend will be replicated.

Usually people don't just wake up one morning and decide to kill themselves; there is generally a history of threat or hints that suicide is an option. In my experience, if the person has some rudimentary plan such as time, place and method, then the threat is very real and you would be wise to obtain professional help as quickly as possible. Here are some further suggestions that may help you cope whilst you are securing professional support:

Avoid platitudes and treat the issue as very real. Take the person and his declarations as if he means what he says. Do not attempt to negotiate.

Sometimes people commit suicide as a form of retribution or paying back someone else – to make them feel sorry. In such cases do not dwell on that person or how they might react to the intended suicide but rather keep the whole focus of the conversation on the suicidal person.

Give the person your total regard and listen to him – using plenty of summary statements – so that you can show in a very real way that you understand his position, feelings and emotions. Many, especially young people, harm themselves because there has been a breakdown in communications with those who are significant in their lives. Coupled with this intense listening, refrain from making any judgemental comments or indeed trying to negotiate or talk them around. They will see what you are doing and you will lose their trust. It is far better to keep them talking until they are all talked out.

If it looks as if the person really is going to kill himself then you move from being non-directive and get the person to hospital or a crisis centre and/or notify the police as soon as possible. Tell the person that you understand that he is in real psychological pain but that this will pass with time and that he must hang on and give himself a chance. This is the only area where you will not be expected to be bound by the confidentiality protocols. You have every right to prevent someone harming himself or others and this overrides any contract you have with the individual. Once the event is over and the person is safe you will enjoy his positive regard again, which is worth all possible irrational anger at the time.

COPING MECHANISMS FOR CLIENTS IN CRISIS

What follows are some very quick 'band-aids' which you can try with your client when and where appropriate. They are not magic, nor is there a guarantee that any one works. You have to be flexible and creative in their usage depending on the person, the situation and the direction you want to go.

The real danger is to become platitudinous or make suggestions which are clearly inappropriate given the situation.

1) Give the problem a number: humans are great at scaling things. For example, right now on a scale of 1 (lowest) to 10 (highest), how happy are you? How fit are you? How comfortable are you? Most people would not experience difficulty in allocating a number to the questions. In much the same way difficulties can be given a number and if it is anything less than 10 then you know, and more importantly the client knows, that they have coped with worse things before. Why not a 10? How did you cope when you faced a 10?

2) What is the gift that the problem brings with it? Most people looking back on a difficulty or a problem in retrospect discover they learnt or achieved something because of their hardship. This was the gift. What is the gift hidden in the present unfortunate situation?

3) Act as if nothing has happened: in shock some people do this anyway as a mechanism of delaying their trauma until such time as they are ready to deal with it. It is sometimes called psychic defence – you can only take what you can take. If clients just concentrate on what to do next and ignore the current pain they frequently can pull themselves through the crisis. Like soldiers wounded on the battlefield who are too busy to take notice of their injuries, some act as if the pain was not there.

4) Worse comparison: situations could always be made worse and providing you keep this in the realms of reality and put your statements in the positive, clients realize their good fortune in the midst of their misery.

'Fortunately you have supportive parents'

'It must be a relief to know that your wife works'
'You are lucky to have kept your health through all this'
'At least you don't have . . . worries'

Very few people indeed end up like Job who lost his
wealth, his health, his family, and sat, covered in sores,
on a dung heap being challenged by his friends who
were convinced that he must have done something
wrong to deserve all his misery.

5) Give genuine praise to the client: this is a well-
known bedside manner technique used by doctors to
motivate their patients. 'I never thought I would see you
walking like that', to someone with a double hip
replacement, or 'You are so positive, I'm really proud of
you', to someone with a degenerative disease. As a counsellor you too can make positive statements of praise:

'You have coped very well . . .'
'I'm surprised you have come through it so well'
'Others would have thrown in the towel long ago'
'You set an example to us all'
'I think you are wonderful for not giving in'
'You are a credit to your family'

Having 'coped well' it is difficult for the person not to
cope and similarly, 'to have come through it well' makes
it difficult to 'go back to it'. Obviously the praise has to
pass the face validity test and be delivered straight from
the heart with honesty and integrity.

PART 4

Capturing success

REJOICING IN THE SMALL SUCCESSES

Counselling is very much like a tug of war. You first help the client to hang on, for no one has the strength to pull all the time. Then when there is a give in the right direction you help the client pull as hard as he can and secure his new ground by digging in and resting again. It is rare that problems facing the client are 'pulled away' all at once.

So when clients tell you of successes, however minor, they are not only to be congratulated and rewarded but also invited to explore how their success has come about.

'Exactly what did you do?'
'How did it help?'
'How did it make you feel?'
'What helped?'
'How did you manage it?'
'What was different?'
'What will you do next time?'

All the questions, delivered in a positive manner can

help your client understand and enjoy his success. Remind him that what he thought difficult and over-whelming is now being managed. New behaviour often forms a bridgehead to resolution of the problem.

It is very important for the client to appreciate that he was the agent of change. It was his success, not luck or some fortuitous happenstance that effected the result. Sometimes clients will attribute success to you, the coun-sellor, and flattering as this might be it is appropriate to reflect this back to the client. You did not make it hap-pen, they did, your role was merely one of facilitator. Our role is to make our client independent of us. We have a vested interest in saying goodbye to clients.

Having said all this it is also important to ensure that changes are kept in perspective. Frequently clients take two steps forward and one and a half steps back shortly after. The road to heaven in counselling is paved with small changes with the client in control and focusing on the future. (See the notes on giving genuine praise in the Coping with Crisis section.)

FROM THE SPECIFIC TO THE GENERAL

What is important is for clients to gain confidence in their own ability and as that ability grows so they can move to even bigger opportunities. If they have improved their relationship, control, or reduced their fear, anger or anxiety in a situation, how can they use that new empowerment in other similar situations? Don't stay on 'the ground floor' but move upwards to discover possibilities of solutions to other difficulties.[26]

How could they move from the specific one-off

[26] Haron, J, *Helping the Client*, Sage (1990)

success to a contest of continual successes? If they can banish the darkness in one part of their life through turning on the light, what other switches are there to be discovered and turned on? Where else would light be helpful? Which areas might they try to illuminate first, second and third?

CLIENT HEAL YOURSELF

Letting your clients go and helping them to be independent of you when appropriate is just as important as being skilled at counselling. If we are true to the Rogerian shibboleths of empathy, positive unconditional regard and genuineness then we will encourage clients to help themselves – first by participating in the therapeutic process and then by managing as much of the process as they are able. This has been called 'guided self-change'. Once the initial crisis or pain has passed most people are capable of helping themselves and should be encouraged to do so. They can be given homework or projects, asked to maintain a log of their activities and behaviours. Some therapists get their clients to talk to themselves on tape and then listen to themselves, working towards self-explanations, options and possible future directions or trailing new behaviour.

In all of this it is important for tasks and 'homework' to be perceived as relevant and appropriate by the client. Sometimes, as counsellors we assign work which we are attached to or have found value from which may not be appropriate to the specific requirements of the client.[27]

[27] Sutherland, S, in Dryden, W and Feltham, C (Eds) *Psychotherapy and its Discontents*, Milton Keynes: Open University Press (1992)

SAYING GOODBYE

You cannot stay with your clients for ever. Obvious as this may sound, clients as well as yourself, must prepare for the separation. The secondary benefits of counselling are considerable, especially when you have been successful together. Sometimes clients will treat you as a talisman, or rabbit's foot – they can be successful providing they can come and see you regularly. Counselling is a means to an end and not an end in itself, as enjoyable as it may be.

There are various tactics you can employ to facilitate the break.

- Have 'follow-up meetings' rather than formal sessions with your client.
- Talk openly about having achieved the original goals and thus the contract is coming to a natural conclusion.
- Have your meetings less frequently.
- Talk to your client about how they might feel when they no longer have to come and see you.
- Move to telephone counselling or seeing the client 'off-site' in more 'natural' surroundings.
- Invite the client to write a 'goodbye' letter and you can do the same.

By being flexible you can wean the client towards full autonomous empowerment.

The greatest compliment I can ever receive from a client goes something like this:

'It has been really good to work with you and I have enjoyed our sessions, but on reflection I think I could have done it on my own.'

'You *could honour me as your teacher by ceasing to be my student.*'[28]
  Nietzsche

[28] Nietzsche, F, Letters. In W. Kaufman (Trans) *The Portable Nietzsche*, Princeton University Press (1968)

Taking it further

Skills workshops can be an excellent way of developing one's counselling skills. This introductory book, of necessity, cannot cover all aspects of counselling but it does describe the way I work. Reading the book is not as effective as learning within a small group programme where skills can be modelled and trialled. Also, participants find that workshops increase personal confidence and encourage 'best practice' activity.

If you would like more information about the training programmes we have designed for such organizations as the BBC, AWE and the British Council please write or call:

UK: Transcareer
    94 High Street
    Lindfield
    West Sussex RH16 2HP
    Tel: (44) 01444 483057
    Fax: (44) 01444 484867

Australia: Transcareer
Level 2
71 York Street
Sydney
NSW 2000
Tel: (61) 02 299 8699
Fax: (61) 02 299 8735

PERFECT COMMUNICATIONS

Andrew Leigh and Michael Maynard

Taking for their main topics impact, spoken communication, group communication, honesty, feedback, building relationships, telephone and written communication, creativity and conflict resolution, the authors pilot the reader swiftly and surely through the do's and don'ts and provide all the information necessary to ensure that communications will be perfect whatever the subject and whoever one is communicating with.

£6.99   0 09 941006 0

PERFECT TIME MANAGEMENT

Ted Johns

Managing your time effectively means adding value to everything you do. This book will help you to master the techniques and skills essential to grasping control of your time and your life.

If you can cut down the time you spend meeting people, talking on the 'phone, writing and reading business papers and answering subordinates' questions, you can use the time saved for creative work and the really important elements of your job. Learn how to deal with interruptions, manage the boss and cut down on meetings time – above all, how to minimize paperwork. You'll be amazed how following a few simple guidelines will improve the quality of both your working life and your leisure time.

£6.99   0 09 941004 4

THE PERFECT BUSINESS PLAN

Ron Johnson

A really professional business plan is crucial to success. This book provides a planning framework and shows you how to complete it for your own business in 100 easy to follow stages.

Business planning will help you to make better decisions today, taking into account as many of the relevant factors as possible. A carefully prepared business plan is essential to the people who will put money into the business, to those who will lend it money, and above all to the people who carry out its day to day management.

£6.99   0 09 941005 2

THE PERFECT PRESENTATION

Andrew Leigh and Michael Maynard

Many people are terrified of making a presentation in public, while others are just unsure of how to go about it effectively. But the ability to do it successfully can make all the difference to your personal career, and to the business prospects of your firm. This book provides a sure-fire method based on the 5 P's of Perfect Presentation: Preparation, Purpose, Presence, Passion and Personality. It is an excellent, hands-on-guide which takes the reader step by step to success in one of the most important business skills.

£6.99   0 09 941002 8